D1195834

FINLAND: A NATION OF CO-OPERATORS

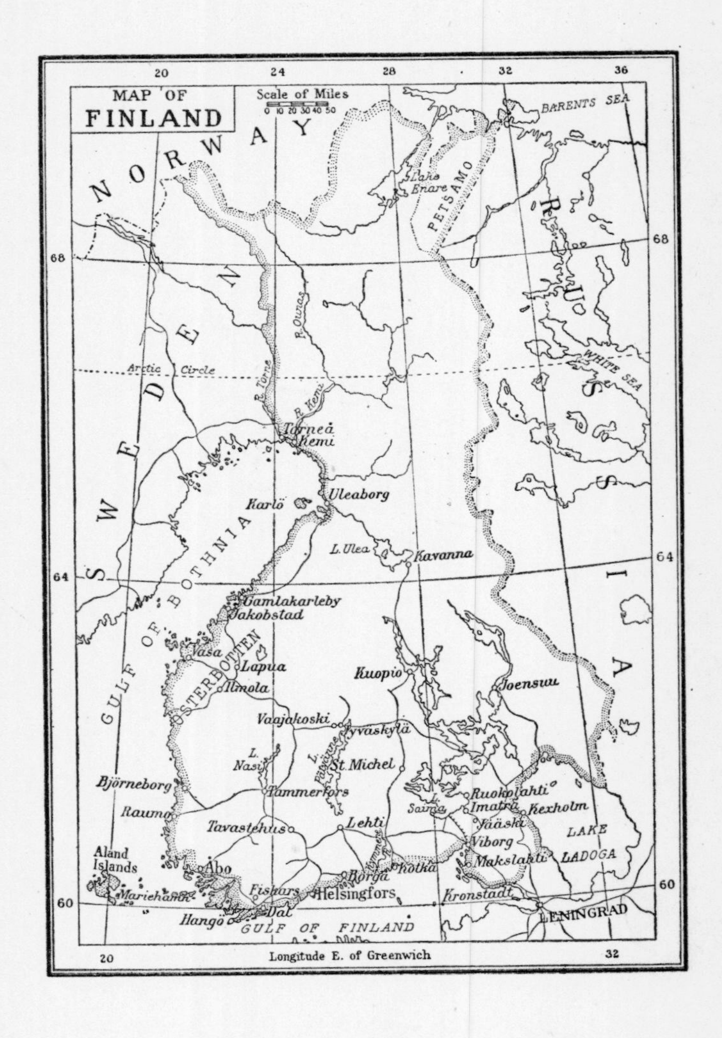
MAP OF
FINLAND
Scale of Miles
0 10 20 30 40 50
NORWAY
SWEDEN
RUSSIA
BARENTS SEA
WHITE SEA
PETSAMO
Lake Enare
R. Ounas
R. Torne
R. Kemi
Arctic Circle
Tornea
Kemi
Uleaborg
Karlö
L. Ulea
Kavanna
GULF OF BOTHNIA
ÖSTERBOTTEN
Gamlakarleby
Jakobstad
Vasa
Lapua
Ilmola
Kuopio
Joensuu
Vaajakoski
Jyvaskylä
L. Nasi
L. Päijänne
St. Michel
Björneborg
Tammerfors
Ruokolahti
Imatra
Kexholm
Rauma
L. Saima
Jääski
Tavastehus
Lehti
LAKE LADOGA
Viborg
Aland Islands
Abo
Borga
Kotka
Makslahti
Mariehamn
Fiskars
Helsingfors
Kronstadt
LENINGRAD
Hangö
Dal
GULF OF FINLAND
20
24
28
32
36
68
64
60
Longitude E. of Greenwich

FINLAND:

A NATION OF CO-OPERATORS

BY

THORSTEN ODHE

Translated from the Swedish by

JOHN DOWNIE

LONDON
WILLIAMS & NORGATE LTD.
1931

PRINTED IN GREAT BRITAIN BY
UNWIN BROTHERS LIMITED, LONDON AND WOKING

CONTENTS

TRANSLATOR'S NOTE

To those, the great majority, who think of Finland, if at all, as an icy waste on the fringe of civilisation, these pages will prove an astonishing revelation. With characteristic enterprise the Swedish Co-operative Union despatched Mr. Odhe to Finland to investigate for Swedish co-operators and farmers the success of Finnish Co-operation. The result is a book that should be of much service to any country whose agriculture is in need of rescue, and that applies to most of Europe.

Since the excellent work of Professor Gebhard, issued by this firm in 1916, on Co-operation in Finland, immense progress has been made, but not until now published, except in confusing snatches, to English readers. That gap is now filled by Mr. Odhe, the great merit of whose contribution of necessity suffers in translation, but remains still notable.

While names more familiar to British readers have been retained for towns and places, the Finnish names, where applicable, have been preferred for the various co-operative movements and agencies. Since repetition of many of these would be cumbrous and meaningless, in general they will, after one full mention, be indicated by their initials. Values and quantities have been anglicised, except that the ton, unless otherwise noted, is the metric ton of 2,204 English lb.

J. D.

AUTHOR'S FOREWORD

Co-operation in Finland ranks among the most successful applications of that principle to trade and business by an entire nation that our day can show.

Finnish people are naturally patient and contented, and their material progress was long held in check by the unfavourable and even odious conditions in which they were doomed to live. A cultured race, reared in the Swedish fold, they seemed fated to lose their whole identity under the spiritually and materially stifling Czardom. In that plight co-operation proved a means of salvation whereby resistance to such annihilation might be organised and democracy rescued.

That was thirty years ago, and in the interval co-operation in Finland has advanced with giant strides, till now it is among the most progressive of modern States, with industries solidly based on natural resources allied with thriving cottage industry. The grandchildren of the "squatters", the old shiftless dregs of an agricultural population, so aptly described by the great Finnish poet Runeberg, have become a race of keen, foresighted, intelligent smallholders, striving earnestly to achieve independence and comfort.

Increasing numbers find employment in factory and workshop. Co-operative organisation has exceeded all expectations in minimising expenses for the country population and increasing their sales returns, swinging the whole of production to where it is required, and therefore profitable. Finland bids fair to become a leader in Europe in smallholdings and in creamery productions. Consumer co-operation has kept down the cost of living, thus immensely strengthening competitive effectiveness in the world markets.

The national discipline ingrained in the Finn during his years of passive and obstinate resistance to Russian influence facilitates now efficient supervision over co-operation's many fields, systematic co-ordination of forces, and appropriate centralisation under full democratic control. Only so was Finnish Co-operation after the World War, and the costly achievement of national independence, able to carry on, and to save the fragments of its sadly shrunk resources against and for the time and process of reconstruction.

This book is mainly the result of a visit of investigation in 1929. Co-operators in Finland of every variety and experience readily and lavishly assisted the writer to discover the great part that co-operation has played, and continues to play, in the evolution of modern Finland. And when the book was printed they very generously revised the proof to verify facts and figures, and to correct errors and misapprehensions—a tedious task. To all, the writer takes this opportunity of tendering his warmest thanks.

Any service the book may yield is very largely to be ascribed to the kind help of these friends. For any faults or errors the author is alone to blame.

T. O.

PLACE-NAMES IN FINNISH AND SWEDISH

SWEDISH	FINNISH
BJÖRNEBORG	PORI
BORGÅ	PORVOO
FINLAND	SUOMI
GAMLAKARLEBY	KOKKOLA
HANGÖ	HANKO
HELSINGFORS	HELSINKI
ILMOLA	ILMAJOKI
JAKOBSTAD	PIETERSAARI
JÄÄSKI	JÄÄSKIS
KEMI	KIMITO
KYMMENE R.	KYMINJOKI
LAPPO	LAPUA
LEHTI	LAHTIS
MARIEHAMN	MAARIANHAMINA
RAUMO	RAUMA
ST. MICHEL	MIKKELI
TAMMERFORS	TAMPERE
TAVASTEHUS	HÄMEENLINNA
TORNEÅ	TORNIO
ULEÅBORG	OULU
VIBORG	VIIPUURI
ÅBO	TURKU
ÅMINNE	JOENSUU

Most of the other places mentioned have no second name.

ANNUAL AVERAGE EQUIVALENT OF £1 IN FINNISH MARKS, 1914—1929

YEAR	MARKS
1914	25·99
1915	31·29
1916	34·30
1917	35·00
1918	39·40
1919	66·97
1920	105·44
1921	199·18
1922	205·88
1923	171·10
1924	176·23
1925	191·86
1926	193·02
1927	193·09
1928	193·32
1929	193·11

From BANK OF FINLAND YEAR BOOK, 1929

Conversion into British equivalent values is made throughout on this basis. In years of violent fluctuation the figures resulting are therefore only approximate.

FINLAND: A NATION OF CO-OPERATORS

CHAPTER I

GENERAL CONDITIONS IN FINLAND

The development and success of co-operation in Finland will be better appreciated following a brief account of the economic life and resources of the country. With these, indeed, co-operation is, of course, inseparably intertwined, and with economic and social progress, phenomenally rapid in recent years. An uninterrupted and systematic reciprocity between co-operative effort on the one hand, and the promotion and improvement of agriculture, dairying, forestry, cattle-rearing, small credit provision, insurance, trade and industrial production on the other, has been characteristic of Finland more perhaps than of any other country in Europe. And in no other country has the co-operative movement found such general acceptance by all classes as a means of utilising the nation's resources more rationally, and of raising the standard of the people both material and moral.

NATURAL CONDITIONS AND DISTRIBUTION OF POPULATION

Finland is poorly favoured by nature. "Our land is poor, so shall be", sang Runeberg eighty years ago. They who have tended the economic development of Finland since that day have never been allowed to forget that first phrase even when they were little disposed to accept the second. Incessant toil, patience, and mobilisation of all available forces have been needed so that out of Finland's scanty natural wealth might be wrung the comparatively high standard of living and the high degree of civilization the nation can now show. Finland's achievement is possibly without parallel in history, handicapped as she was by wretched poverty and political oppression and repression.

Geographically, Finland lies wholly North of the latitude of Leningrad, and extends to that of the North Cape. Of the total area, not far short of Great Britain and Ireland, 11·5 per cent. is water. "The land of the thousand lakes" is no poetic exaggeration; the Ordnance Survey map shows 35,500. About 6·3 per cent. of the land only is under tillage, in the northern provinces 1 per cent.; natural meadows and pasture account for 3·6 per cent., and the remainder, 90·1 per cent., consists of forests, scrub and uncultivable. The population is in the neighbourhood of 3,500,000, thus no more than 27 to the square mile. North Finland consists of vast forest tracts with very few inhabitants.

Only along the coast, and in a few scattered areas inland, are there centres of population and cultivated tracts of any extent. Still, agriculture has always been, and is yet, Finland's principal occupation; about two-thirds of the people subsist on agriculture and allied industries. The remainder are engaged in factories, transport, trade, seafaring, public service, and in the professions. That scientific forestry takes pride of place in industry is, therefore, not surprising. Saw-mills and the manufacture of wood-pulp and paper increase apace in Finland, and support an ever-growing corps of workers. In saw-milling, Finland leads Europe; its timber exports have lately been the largest in the world, and still rank with those of the United States of America, Canada, and Sweden.

Progress has not been confined to forest industries; those working up raw material for the home market—

textiles, machinery, boots, leather—have long existed, and, despite post-war difficulties, the Finnish home-market industries have been able to hold their own to such purpose that most of the demand in the common necessities, such as boots, clothing, household utensils, etc., can be met from home factories.

The immense water power available in its falls will certainly, when more fully utilised, considerably accelerate industrialisation, already rapid. Helsingfors (221,000), Åbo (63,000), Tammerfors (53,000), Viborg (50,000), with a string of smaller towns such as Vasa, Kuopio, Uleåborg, Björneborg, Kotka, Lehti, Jakobstad, are all potential industrial centres, but in purely rural areas also exist quite a number of smaller communities congregated each round a mill or a factory. Twenty per cent. only of the population dwell in towns and their suburbs.

The Rapid Development of Finnish Agriculture

Agriculture, the premier industry of Finland, has made phenomenal progress, mechanical and commercial, in the last generation. Not so long ago brush-burning was an essential part of tillage. The simple implements and methods of that time are little more than a memory now.

Of the acreage under crops, one-third is grain, 3 to 4 per cent. potatoes, about half in hay and other fodder, indicating how important forage-cropping and dairy-farming have become in Finland's agricultural economy. Besides the cultivated grazing there is extensive natural pasture.

Still grain-cropping remains sufficient to meet the greater part of home bread needs. Thus in 1929, 358,000 tons of native rye were produced against rye imports of 201,000 tons. Wheat is little grown, but increasingly consumed—at the expense of rye; so imports in 1929, all as flour, came to 137,000 tons, while home crops yielded 32,000 tons. Some barley is grown and used in places for bread; and oats-growing has so much increased that very little feeding meal is now imported. All this is the more creditable in that frost ever remains a serious menace; in 1923, and again in 1928, northern districts suffered severely.

Development, however, as stated, favours forage-cropping, and this in time has led to more rotation of crops, and to increased acreage under clover and legumes, adding to the fertility of the soil under cultivation. The opinion is general that in such ways up to 75 per cent. of home bread needs can for a long time to come be met by home supplies.

Deeper tillage, better drainage, and improved seed strains are all being sedulously pursued and practised to increase output per acre and diminish frost risk. Farm manure, once little heeded, is now carefully husbanded and applied. Moorland and marsh, of which about one-third of the land surface consists, are being steadily nibbled by tillage to help the nation's food supply. Possibly no country in Europe is so rich in untouched potential farm land.

In dairy produce Finland supplies many besides her own, and in growing numbers. Cattle are increasing rapidly, and horses for lumbering. Artisans and labourers keep cows, as well as peasants and farmers. These "town cows" are summer-grazed on rented pasture or on the town common, and fed in winter on bought hay. Averaging 2,850 to 3,100 lb. per cow, the country's total milk production is reckoned at 16,000,000 to 19,000,000 tons a year. Although export continues to expand, much is retained for home consumption. Very little margarine is as yet eaten in Finland. Creamery butter production in 1928 amounted to 21,000 tons; cheese production to 4,500 tons.

A Land of Smallholders

The conditions of land ownership peculiar to Finland have contributed largely to the diversion of production in the direction of dairy-farming and its subsidiaries: poultry, eggs, honey, pig-feeding, etc. Always a nation of smallholders, this feature has of late become even more pronounced. Of 250,000 holdings in 1920 exceeding 1¼ acres under cultivation, 182,000 were owned by the occupiers, 68,000 rented. Of the whole 250,000 there were:

38·5 per cent. less than 7¼ acres each
39·2 per cent. between 7¼ and 24¾ acres each
16·4 per cent. between 24¾ and 61¾ acres each
4·4 per cent. between 61¾ and 123 acres each
0·4 per cent. more than 250 acres each

There are whole counties consisting exclusively of smallholders, and the general tendency is in that direction. The larger farms, very useful in their day for trying out new methods and machinery, are passing into the hands of peasants, or being divided amongst next-of-kin, or being purchased by State or commune for land-settlement purposes.

Over 130,000 independent holdings were created by the release of cottars from service obligations to the farmers and landowners from whom they held. An Act of 1918 endowed them with these holdings as their own. And land settlement, or home colonisation, beginning about 1880, has been rapidly accelerated these last ten years, over 30,000 new holdings being created. State, local authorities, colonisation committees, and co-operative credit banks all lend their aid.

The number of smallholdings has thus been increased beyond 300,000, *supporting a population of* 1,200,000 *or* 40 *per cent. of the whole nation.*

The obvious appeal of co-operation to smallholders has been fully recognised, and thereby, indeed, has been imparted the new impetus and direction to production, especially typified in dairying development. This co-operation is no more than a modernised version of the long-practised mutual help common in districts where smallholding is of ancient standing whenever any work fell to be done which was beyond the powers of the holder and his family. These casual associations for building, clearing, ploughing, harvesting had well prepared the way for more permanent co-operation.

Forest Industries

After Russia, Finland is Europe's richest country in timber; relatively to population she is, indeed, the richest. Of forests she has over 60,000,000 acres—slightly more than Sweden, and almost twice Germany, the two next following in forest acreage. The export of timber and tar is centuries old. 1860–70 saw the first modern saw-mill, and the appearance of the three letters D.B.B. (deals, boards, battens) in Finnish export statistics. Big saw-mills sprang up at river mouths and lake outlets, such as those of Ahlström and Rosenlew in Björneborg, the Uleåborg Company in the town of that name, the Kemi Company in Kemi, etc.

At the mouth of the historic Kymmene River a new town arose, American fashion, almost overnight, when the Norwegian firm Gultzeit & Company in 1918 began saw-milling there. This business has since been acquired by the State, now one of the biggest timber traders. Cellulose and paper manufacture followed. Progress has been especially rapid since the war. The same firms engage in all these industries, and own besides vast timber tracts the offal from which is used in the latter industries, which thus complete the exploitation of the timber resources. Finland has cellulose and paper factories among the largest and most modern in Europe.

Manufacture of furniture, building material, cases, bobbins, spools, veneers, carries the timber nearer to practical use, and, while reducing freights, increases values of exports. Pine, fir, and birch are all freely used, so that Finland's birch-groves are more than a charming feature of the landscape, and a delight to the tourist. The match industry, using much poplar wood, also belongs in large part to the timber group.

Figures show what timber means to Finland. Nearly 50 per cent. of the value of the total industrial production is the contribution from timber and its subsidiaries; 76,000 are employed against 93,600 in all other industrial occupations. Many smallholders and landless labourers also eke out their livelihood with winter timber-felling. Of 1929 exports, amounting in total value to some £33,000,000, timber, woodwork, cardboard, and paper accounted for over 85 per cent. In sawn and planed wood Finland is since the war among the world's foremost exporters, supplying as much as 1¼ million standards in some years compared to Sweden's 1 million.

While this exceeds the natural increment of timber growth, meantime the abundance of mature wood is being cleared for replanting. The annual growth is estimated at over 1,500 million cubic feet, which can be substantially increased by drainage and scientific attention. Much wood is used for fuel in coalless Finland; railway locomotives, for example, are largely stoked with wood.

Home Industries: Textiles and Engineering Lead

Though much smaller in comparison, other industries are of great national importance. Cotton, wool, and linen manufactures, centred in Tammerfors—Finland's Manchester—supply by far the most of home requirements to the value of £6,200,000 in 1927, and indeed formerly exported in fair quantity to Russia. Some of the factories, for example the century-old Finlayson's, rank amongst the largest in Scandinavia. Shoe and leather industries, similarly sufficient, are found also in Tammerfors, and in Uleåborg and elsewhere, producing to the value of £2,350,000 in the same year.

Another important group is the metal and engineering trades. Several ironworks, notably Fiskars and Dals, in South Finland, have existed since the sixteenth century, and still turn out ploughs and implements. Lacking native ore, Finnish engineering has to depend on foreign supplies, including Swedish high-grade steel for machine tools. Against textiles' 23,000, this group employs also 23,000 workers, turning out nails, cast-iron, building fitments, ploughs, picks, spades, threshing mills, and other agricultural machinery, separators, machine tools, boilers, steam-engines, petrol-motors, locomotives, and railway carriages, etc., to the value in 1928 of £8,300,000. Specialising to home requirements, especially in agricultural and lumbering tools and machinery, Finland's engineering stands fast against severe foreign competition, and promises healthy growth. Russia in former times was quite a good market for Finland's engineering.

Other successful home industries include tobacco manufacture with £2,260,000 production in 1928; milling, formerly discouraged by the Russians who wished to preserve Finland as a market for Russian flour; and baking. While small village mills are still numerous, and little wheat is imported whole, there is every prospect of early and extensive co-operative invasion of the milling industry.

Co-operative bakeries are much the largest and most modern in the country. Finland's bakery production in 1928 was about £1,840,000. Margarine is manufactured in Finland to the extent of 6½ lb. per head of the population per annum, against 20 in Sweden, and several times that even in Denmark. Even that small quantity diminishes when butter prices fall. Co-operation has invaded this domain also where probably the next few years will see much expansion.

Finland's "White Coal"

By skilful adaptation to needs and close attention to quality, Finland has contrived to retain the tight hold she secured on the home market during the war with its shortage.

Still, most progress seems likely in the near future from the export industries. Finland's first economist, Anders Chydenius, wrote, over a hundred and fifty years ago: "A nation does not gain by multiplying the variety of its interests and occupations, but by concentrating on the most profitable, on those in which the least number of men produce the highest value in goods." Her bounteous stores of timber indicate emphatically the path of Finland's future industrial development. The power problem is simple; 2½ to 3 million h.p. of water awaits harness, possible of fourfold multiplication, by damming and regulation.

As yet a mere beginning has been made, but that includes Imatra, the richest power waterfall in Europe, with a power station capable of 70,000 kilovoltamperes, which can be increased to 150,000 when required. A cable carrying 110,000 volts runs from Imatra to Abo, 230 miles, with a branch, among several, to Helsingfors. Rural electrification advances rapidly; 55 per cent. of the 537 communes have been supplied at a cost of £5,200,000. High and low-tension cables are a common feature in the landscape of south and mid Finland; a great number of small low-tension substations serve villages and farms. Even here co-operation is active both in construction and in operation work. But Finland is still much behind Sweden, Norway, and Switzerland in the utilisation of its water resources.

"Our Land is Poor"—in Capital

Ever since the war Finland has been short of capital. That calamity and the Civil War in Finland which followed annihilated the value of the Finnish mark, and so made extremely difficult both home capitalisation and foreign accommodation. And so far as foreign capital is shy or is declined, definite limits are imposed on the development of her great natural resources.

Stabilisation of the mark by the Act of December 21, 1925, at 39·70 to the dollar (193·23 to the £), as against 5·14 in 1914, assisted notably domestic accumulation and foreign sympathy. In all about £31,500,000 has been borrowed abroad since 1918; half for the conversion of existing loans. But the need for capital is still great.

Of late there has been considerable improvement in roads and transport, and in reducing the deficiency of housing—a natural sequel to the new conditions and impulse springing from political independence and economic revival.

A Finnish economist calculates that in the period 1918–28 the capital expenditure in agriculture and its related industries has been £46,600,000; in export industries, £20,700,000; in other sale industries, £10,400,000. Transport and postal services have been improved by £18,100,000; electrical and other trade and industry by £10,400,000. On buildings and furnishing other than agricultural has been expended £25,900,000, and on public buildings, hospitals, schools, barracks, etc., £7,800,000. These approximate figures, totalling nearly £140,000,000, give an idea of the powerful national forces released when this little country joined the ranks of the world's free nations.

From 1921–9 Finland's exports increased almost twofold—to £33,300,000—and imports in like degree, the latter consisting largely of building material, raw material and machinery for manufacture, and, in increasing quantities, of consumption goods. Imports reached £41,500,000 in 1928, dropping back to £35,100,000 in 1929. Thus the economic development has substantially raised the standard of living. Motors, motor-cycles, wireless, and gramophones reach ever further down the social scale. Withal saving has not been neglected; 1920–9 deposits in private banks exactly doubled, up to £38,800,000, while those of the small savings institutions increased more than twice as fast—from £5,700,000 to £25,900,000.

The saving habit has always been a Finnish trait, largely indeed out of sheer necessity in so poor a country. Inflation dissipated nine-tenths of the value of all savings, a heavy blow to frugality, which makes its recovery all the more remarkable.

That much of the increase in the national income should go to improvement of the standard of living appears less strange remembering the low standard previously obtaining, far below what was appropriate to Finland's degree of civilisation. Foreign capital will be necessary for still some time to come, for large-scale industry and in public enterprise, while the needs of agriculture can be met, at least mainly, from home savings, thanks very largely to co-operative effort.

Economic Development, Character, Education

Natural resources and available capital do not alone decide a nation's economic fate; the national character plays a very important part.

In ability and application, and in the will and the

power to acquire knowledge and training, the Finnish stand particularly high. The Nordic strain cannot be denied, and indeed is freely considered to exceed the Swedish element, represented now by 11 per cent. Swedish-speaking along the Baltic coast, and relatively diminishing. Language signifies little in this case; anthropometric measurement and biological examination have proved the importance of the Nordic strain in Finland's development.

Finnish temperament and national capacities exhibit convincingly the far-reaching and beneficial effects of this blend of races. To the purely Finnish industry, hardihood, endurance, and patience (Finland's staying power has commanded respect and admiration on fields other than the running-track) have been allied the Nordic passion for independence and for democratic forms of society and depth of feeling. Love of education and learning, and the power quickly to grasp and apply book knowledge, are vivid national traits, as also are the gift and appreciation of poetry and music.

In the sixteenth century, when yet Sweden ruled, the bishopric of Åbo, including most of Finland's population, bore the palm for popular education in all the Swedish Kingdom. Illiteracy has long been practically non-existent: schools will compare with any in Europe. Technical and agricultural education have always been zealously promoted, and folk schools in the country and workers' institutes in the towns have rendered incalculable service in adult and economic education in co-operation and in communal and political life.

Finnish higher education and scientific activity have long enjoyed considerable fame in Europe, as many eminent names bear witness. Never the least exclusive, higher education has seen its mission in the diffusion of knowledge among the whole people and in their uplift. Neither the present development of agriculture, nor that of industry, is conceivable in Finland without general appreciation of its direction and goal, or without close organisation and co-ordination of forces, the fruits of the high national cultural level attained. The same factor has contributed lavishly to the spread of the co-operative movement, in which, indeed, apostles of popular education have borne a noble share.

Finland thus can show a really democratic trade and life, and therewith a vigorous development of public enterprise. All railways belong to the State; practically all gas, water, and electricity supplies in towns and larger communities are publicly owned, and much of the autobus traffic. The manufacture of requirements for the Army and for public authorities is a State or semi-State undertaking, and even in production for sale the State and local authorities take active and considerable part.

While difference of opinion may exist as to the nature and extent of public enterprise and trading most advantageous to the nation, there is general unanimity in favour of increasing democratic control of trade, and its removal from the arena of political strife—an opinion shared by the whole co-operative movement in Finland. In the fullest sense of the word that movement has always been national, building up national solidarity, lifting the whole race on to a higher plane, material, spiritual, even cultural, training the people in the fuller utilisation of their powers, especially economic, and, so, intimately and essentially involved in the general development of trade and culture.

CHAPTER II

SCOPE OF CO-OPERATION IN FINLAND

In most countries co-operative societies and the movement generally shot up first in a promiscuous and spontaneous fashion, and formed their central organisations later. Thus in England they were originally the unpremeditated expression of the self-help efforts of industrial workers in the Hungry Forties, and not until a generation later did they combine for wholesale supply.

But in Finland co-operation mainly progressed along lines quite other—according to a definite, preconceived plan, from an established centre outwards. Thus, from the very beginning, system and method characterised and expedited the development of Finnish co-operation. This central institution—the Pellervo Society—so directed and co-ordinated effort that the most effective co-operative use was made of power and resources.

First Beginnings

In 1866 Professor Palmén made the first known attempt to found a consumer co-operative society in Finland. Acquaintance with the English co-operative movement had fired him with a desire that his class might pioneer a similar venture in his own country, at once to eke out their own scanty means and to set example to the workers and the poorer classes. He delivered an address that attracted some attention, rules were devised, and canvassing lists were opened, but the response froze off any further action.

Occasional notices and articles continued to appear in the Press, evincing particularly interest in Swedish attempts at organised co-operation, and in 1878 another start was made, this time by the workers employed by the Viborg Engineering Company, on the instigation of the managing director, Törnroth, who also had learned to know the co-operative movement in England. This took the form of a joint-stock company.

A similar business was commenced in Tammerfors, followed in 1883 in Helsingfors by the first to introduce the members' single equal vote. In 1889 Helsingfors saw its first open consumer co-operative. By this time many of the towns had business undertakings of more or less co-operative character. The society founded by the workers in Finlayson's factory in Tammerfors in 1900 (the original Finlayson hailed from Glasgow) is frequently mentioned as Finland's first real modern co-operative society, and visitors are still reverently shown its modest "Toad Lane" shop.

Tammerfors's claim is justified by the powerful influence and impetus the society imparted to the infant movement, and because of its prominent part in establishing common and central action and institutions for and by the new co-operatives.

Other attempts about this time were less successful. Many interested agriculturists, for example, issued pamphlets, and strove to create interest among farmers in co-operative dairying, purchasing, etc., but their efforts were little appreciated. Besides, the Russian overlords frowned on any effort to organise the population, scenting political danger and incipient revolution. And not the least of the difficulties was the absence of any law recognising co-operative societies.

The end of last century saw Russian endeavours to suppress Finnish liberties at their worst. In 1898 Bobrikoff was appointed Governor-General especially to speed up Finland's Russification, and the following winter legislation was largely transferred into Russian hands. Some form of resistance was necessary if Finland as a nation was not to disappear altogether. The first step was obviously so to strengthen the economic position of the agricultural population that they would be able to thwart the Russian design of converting Finland into a mere market for Russian produce.

Resistance to Russification: Rise of Co-operation

Much attention was concentrated on this problem, especially among those active in popular education, Their useful labours encountered serious difficulty in the general mean standard of living, and the especially desperate condition of the agricultural class, whose whole energy barely sufficed to keep life alow. Thoughts turned more and more to co-operation, attracted by the success reported from England, Germany, Denmark, and elsewhere. The purely economic basis of co-operation readily commends it to the simplest minds, and this seemed just to fit the needs of Finland at the moment.

Among those thus converted to co-operation was a young member of Helsingfors University staff, Dr. Hannes Gebhard, lecturer in agriculture and Professor 1909–27, who began now seriously to study the small-holder and his possibilities. After much discussion with like-minded, notably Mikael Soininen, later chief of the State Education Department, he decided on a practical start, and on October 2, 1899, the Pellervo Society was formed for the purpose, as stated in the constitution, of "promoting the economic improvement of the people by means of co-operation, and to establish a bond between the various different co-operative societies in the country".

With the formation of Pellervo—so named after the god of Fertility and Good Harvest in Kalevala, the national epic—systematic co-operation begins in Finland. Dr. Gebhard never turned back, and has rendered incalculable service to his countrymen, devoting himself to the movement, and especially to Co-operative Credit Banks. 1899–1917 he was President of Pellervo, and since 1904, except for an interval of four years, he has been managing director of the Central Institute of Co-operative Credit Banks. Professor Gebhard is the real pioneer and founder of Finnish co-operation, and has been its guiding spirit during the last thirty years, and, though still busy in such labours, looks back on a life's work for his country's independence and prosperity that very few can match.

Pellervo's Programme

Pellervo got busy at once with propaganda, model rules, text-books, account-books, assisting and reconciling workers in the co-operative harvest-field, advising enquirers and managements, auditing, compiling statistics, acting as public guardian to all co-operative interests, and custodian of the true co-operative ideals, the practical exploitation of which it left to other organisations. Thus from the very beginning much of the cause of internal conflict was cleverly evaded. No happy chance, but profound study of experience of other countries, underlay Gebhard's plans. During his sojourn abroad in the nineties, particularly in Germany, where he studied under the celebrated Professor Max Sering in Berlin, he had seized the opportunity of examining the various phases of co-operation systematically and in close detail. Already in 1899 he had published his great book in Finnish on *Agricultural Co-operation in other Lands*.

So the one hundred and fifty students despatched early in that year to various parts of Finland to assist in popular education, carried with them the message of the importance of co-operation to the farming class.

Pellervo followed with written and spoken propaganda. Professor Sering had implanted in his pupil the conviction that co-operation was the only hope of the smallholder, and even earlier Gebhard had enthusiastically supported "farmers' guilds", with their educational work and common purchase, as useful introduction to co-operative trading. The efforts of Pellervo, with assistance from agricultural societies, increased the number of these guilds in three years from 60 to 347, and their common purchases amounted to £60,000, a very considerable sum in that day.

The Act of 1901 relating to Co-operative Societies

Gebhard was always convinced that any great progress for co-operative trading required that co-operative societies should be recognised in law. To that end he laboured unceasingly until on March 23, 1899, a Committee of three was appointed, of whom he found himself one, to draft a Bill. The resultant measure was passed in 1900, and came into force September 1, 1901.

The Act allows co-operative associations three different forms of liability: (1) where members have no personal liability and only the Society's own resource can be attached; (2) where members are liable for the Society's obligations, but only to an extent specified in the rules; and (3) where the members are liable without limit on the Society's behalf.

Any one of these three varieties is permissible in any co-operative undertaking whose principal object is to secure economic advantage to its members either by raising their income or by reducing their expenses. Insurance societies are the only exception. Insurance business is prohibited to co-operative societies, a more stable economic basis being considered necessary, and more capital resources than co-operative trading was expected to provide.

The Act signified an immense advance, affording, as it did, protection for every kind of co-operative combination. But of course every possibility could not be guarded. One provision proved later, after war-time inflation, a serious obstacle to financial development. Clause 19 enacts that the written consent of all the members must be given to any increase in the share capital per member to be contributed, and to any addition to the personal liability of the member. Not until 1927 was this amended so that the same purpose could be achieved by a resolution approved at two successive general meetings by majorities of three-fourths of those present and voting.

Another important amendment, passed in 1918, permitted larger societies to substitute delegate meetings for the open general meeting. A second amendment in the same year allowed co-operative central organisations to concede their society members more than one vote in general meeting. Progress and the unforeseen and unexpected had compelled these changes.

The new Act gave fresh and lively impulse to the movement. Up to 1901 only three consumer co-operatives had registered, but in the following year 13 were added, and 28 co-operative creameries, one moss-litter society, and 5 various. By 1903 there were 189 on the register: among them 66 consumer co-operatives, 75 creameries, and 24 Co-operative Credit Banks.

Thus the movement was launched now along three main lines, in touch with each other to such extent that the management consisted often of the same persons: consumer co-operation, creamery co-operation, and credit co-operation. So far consumers' co-operation was limited largely to the industrial workers. By 1903, however, a score of country societies appeared, and in the next two years consumer co-operation spread rapidly in rural Finland, especially after the Big Strike.[1]

In this expansion the main factor was Pellervo's educational propaganda. Its missionaries—agricultural experts, folk-school teachers, and trained business advisers—traversed the country; its handbills and pamphlets circulated in thousands, and its magazine *Pellervo* began a national household invasion.

Here must be emphasised the splendid part played by this magazine, now in its thirtieth year, in Finnish co-operation. Originally it appeared in Finnish and Swedish: now only a Finnish edition is issued. The Swedish edition, during its nineteen years, was edited by Mrs. Hedvig Gebhard, M.P., the worthy helpmate of the Professor on many co-operative fields.

Pellervo's contents include popular articles on co-operative activities, and on agriculture and its related industries, a section for housewives with special regard to country needs, articles on general topics, poetry, and folk-life sketches. The circulation, now 107,000, exceeds that of any other agricultural magazine in Finland or in Scandinavia, and is the more astonishing in that other central co-operative organisations of later origin nearly all publish their own Press, in some cases with circulation running into the hundred thousands.

Possibly no other country can boast a co-operative Press so rich in contents and so wide in circulation as Finland's—a distinction due partly to the high general level of popular education, partly to the great variety of co-operative activity. As the pioneer in this sphere, reaching 23,000 by 1905 and 53,000 in 1915, *Pellervo* deserves special credit.

[1] October 30th to November 6th. Organised in protest against Russian encroachment on Finnish rights. "Red Guard" battalions were formed who desired to call a National Assembly and draft a new Constitution. Eventually the Russian Governor, Prince Obolensky, resigned, and certain violations of Finnish liberties were repealed.

Thirty Years of Pellervo

Prominent among the many offices that Pellervo fills are those of legal consultant, adviser in farm accounting, providing model statements and helpful tables, and guide and instructor in book-keeping, generally with local representatives arranging classes in co-operative theory, and practice for folk-school teachers among others, and compiler and publisher of statistics concerning all forms of co-operative activity. These statistics are published in Pellervo's Year Books, which, excepting for a few years, have been issued both in Finnish and Swedish.

As the various co-operative ventures waxed in strength and self-dependence, and central organisations were created, much of Pellervo's work was transferred thereto, especially as regards the relevant propaganda, which naturally was now undertaken by the respective Central Unions. But Pellervo's programme remains still extensive, and intimate collaboration with these Central Unions ensures the most suitable and advantageous use of its powers and resources for the co-operative movement. For example, its local representatives promote Credit Banks in their districts, carry on creamery propaganda, etc.

With the support of the Central Unions a magazine is published for managers, employees, and committees with a circulation of 4–5,000: *Suomen Osuustoimintalehti* (Finland's *Co-operative News*). The present secretary of Pellervo is Dr. Eemil Hynninen, who served several years with the International Agricultural Institute at Rome, and is counted one of Finland's leading men in agricultural economics and statistics.

The latest figures credit Pellervo with a membership of nearly 1,400 local societies and 7 national organisations—S.O.K., O.K.O., Hankkija, Valio, Muna, and the Cattle and Forestry Centrals, to all of which reference is made later in these pages. Individual membership was discontinued in 1918. The local societies affiliated are, however, only a part of the total in the country—1,372 in 1930, representation being left generally to the national organisations just mentioned.

The rich harvest gleaned through Pellervo is best shown in tabular form:

Year.	Consumer Co-operatives.		Credit Co-operatives.		Creamery Co-operatives.		Others.
	No.	Membership.	No.	Membership.	No.	Membership.	No.
1903	72	13,144	22	521	55	4,025	25
1910	405	79,021	374	17,496	285	30,058	619
1920	623	330,887	616	32,867	345	41,639	1,233
1927	553	412,200	1,399	120,900	664	68,100	2,305
1928	548	432,800	1,427	131,300	676	70,200	1,979

The aggregate number of co-operators in Finland cannot be ascertained by adding these memberships, since many are members of more than one society, a few even of as many as ten societies. Finnish co-operation, especially agricultural, exhibits great luxuriance of variety. In addition to those noted above there are special purchase and sale societies, moss-litter societies, machinery, food grain, and egg sale societies, slaughter-house and milling associations, telephone and land-purchase unions, farmers' guilds, bull societies, control, stallion, and cattle insurance societies, and forestry associations, all more or less co-operative.

And still their number grows. The most notable omission is the co-operative insurance societies with their network of branches and hundreds of thousands of members. These, as mentioned, may not be constituted under the Co-operative Act, but their co-operative character is unassailable. Mention should also be made of Housing Societies, limited companies, but distinctly co-operative in character and aim. Comparatively new, this movement operated in 1928 in 130 societies with 2,200 members.

Ten Central Co-operative Organisations

The various forms of co-operative activity in Finland group themselves now around no less than ten central organisations. The oldest, the Central Institute of the Co-operative Credit Banks (O.K.O., or Osuuskassojen Keskuslainarahasto Osakeyhtiö, in full), was founded in 1902 after the Russian Government had been persuaded by the Finnish Parliament to extend support out of public funds to non-State credit establishments, intended to assist local Co-operative Credit Banks to supply the credit needs of smallholders. In 1903 the first of a series of State loans was granted amounting to £21,000.

Following came the first Finnish Consumer Co-operative Wholesale (S.O.K., or Suomen Osuuskauppojen Keskusosuuskunta Ltd.) in 1904, after long and careful preparation. This began as an advisory and first-aid society, helping local co-operatives to achieve strength and stability, and commencing wholesaling in 1905.

In that year appeared two more federations: Hankkija, a co-operative wholesale for producing agricultural requisites and for the sale of agricultural produce, and Valio for the larger-scale sale of butter, cheese, and general dairy produce from and for affiliated creameries, and in other ways promoting co-operative dairying. Another society, Labor, had existed since 1897 as a common purchasing agency for farmers and estate owners, and was in 1906 converted into a co-operative wholesale in conformity with the Co-operative Act. Labor fulfils the same functions as Hankkija, but limits its operations to the Swedish-speaking population of Finland.

In 1917 the consumers' co-operative movement in Finland was rent in two when most of the societies in towns and industrial centres left S.O.K. and founded their own wholesale OTK (Osuustukkukauppa), having already established a Central Union K.K. (Kulutusosuuskuntien Keskusliitto). Though the latter undertakes publishing and sells office material and furniture, it is not included as a wholesale, more especially as OTK and K.K. are practically one.

The infants of this youthful group of wholesales are those of the Cattle Sale Co-operatives: S.K. (Suomen Karjakeskuskunta) founded 1918; Enigheten (Unity), 1918, the counterpart of Valio in the Swedish-speaking areas, the timber owners: M.M. (Metsänomistajain Metsäkeskus), and the egg-sale central: V.M. (Vientikunta Muna), both 1921.

The total wholesale sales for 1928 approached £15,000,000, excluding, of course, the Credit Banks Institute, with business amounting to about £4,800,000 in the year. The sales of consumer co-operatives reached £16,500,000, while the total turnover of all local societies was £27,000,000. These figures strikingly demonstrate the vast importance attained by the Finnish co-operative movement in thirty years.

The Co-operative a National Movement in Finland

What then has been the general effect of this extensive co-operative organisation and activity? Let us hear the Finns themselves on the subject.

In that great national publication, *Finland: the Country and the People*, issued just after Finland's entry into the circle of free nations, is written: "Recalling the conditions in rural Finland before the advent of the co-operative movement, we remember how painfully dependent were the smallholders and the poorer workers on the middleman and the dealer, who yearly drew millions from the results of their labours. To-day the middleman has almost disappeared. The trade in farm produce has been transferred to a large and increasing extent to the farmers' own trading concerns; consumers supply their own wants, and farmers the requirements of their calling by means of the co-operative society, which further has brought blessing in its train in that it has striven, and with much success, to end the wasteful and disastrous credit trading. Parallel with this development has risen the social influence of the poorer classes. For the status of any section of society in national politics depends finally not so much on its programme and its voting strength as on the service it renders to the commonweal, and it shares in control of the current of social life in proportion as it contributes to the nation's economic and spiritual welfare."

According to the excellent article on Practical Co-operation in the book just mentioned, Co-operation has in Finland become a national movement supported by all classes to an extent hardly conceivable in other countries. Smallholders and those in meaner circumstances are almost completely co-operatised. Indeed, Finland considers that successful and progressive smallholding is quite impossible without co-operative association.

Quoting again from the same source: "But, besides smallholders, the larger farmers and even the wealthier classes have learned the benefits of co-operative effort, just as, on the other hand, smallholders' co-operation requires for its success the sympathy and support of those better circumstanced. In actual fact there are many communes whose inhabitants are almost without exception active co-operators, and in which the co-operative store is the recognised centre for the business and even the cultural life of the commune. In Finland, for example, are to be found a large number of co-operative creameries drawing the milk of every cow in their vicinity. There are some paying annually to their members tens of thousands of pounds for milk supplies, manufacturing butter and cheese, producing electricity for the area's needs, breeding and feeding large numbers of pigs, and lending money to their members for business purposes." And to the industrial worker co-operation has rendered equal service, as we shall learn.

The magnificent development outlined here is amplified in later chapters. Meantime, reference may appropriately be made to two other co-operative organisations devoted to larger co-operative interests and to the promotion of agriculture, colleagues of Pellervo: Finland's Swedish Co-operative Union and the Farmers' Central Union (M.K.).

Finland's Swedish Co-operative Union

This is practically a replica of Pellervo, founded in 1919, and conducting propaganda by lecture and pamphlet, starting new societies, scrutinising rules and schemes of organisation, and directing educational work for Swedish-speaking co-operatives; auditing the accounts of and advising societies not in audit groups as are the consumers' co-operatives and the Credit Banks; publishing co-operative literature for the Swedish-speaking, and watching their interests in the national common bilingual central wholesales and unions.

The Union has now 111 members, mostly local societies, with "Enigheten" and "Labor" Centrals, and all the three creamery unions among the Swedish-speaking. Headquarters are in Helsingfors. The secretary, Ruben Bremer, claims kinship with Frederika Bremer, one of Sweden's most famous women writers, and herself in her day interested in co-operation.

Finland's Swedish Co-operative Union publishes its own newspaper, *Lantmän och Andelsfolk* (*Farmers and Co-operators*), in an issue of 4,000, containing articles on farm management and on the co-operative movement in general, co-operative reports from the Swedish-speaking areas and from Finland generally, with a spicing of fiction and lighter literature and art.

The Union's importance has much increased in recent years. The Swedish element in Finland's population, especially in the country districts, has been considered—rightly or wrongly is of no importance here—distinctly more individualist than the Finnish, in proof of which is cited the readier acceptance and more rapid progress of co-operation among the latter. Lately, however, there has been a surge of improvement in this respect, and to-day the Swedish Co-operative Union of Finland represents about half the Swedish-speaking population, and the largest society as to membership affiliated to S.O.K. is the purely Swedish-speaking "Varuboden" in Helsingfors. The co-operative creamery movement, too, has made rapid strides of late in the three Swedish-speaking creamery districts in West and South Finland, of which more when "Enigheten" comes under review.

MAATALOUSTUOTTAJAIN KESKUSLIITTO, OR M.K.

To give some idea of the work of this Farmers' Central Union mention may first be made that its formation is due to Professor Gebhard and others interested in farming. Early in 1917 Pellervo invited leading farmers to a meeting, where, after discussion, a Central Committee of Agricultural Producers was elected to undertake the starting of local societies. Following this came the inaugural meeting of the Central Union in Helsingfors, September 18, 1917.

The Union undertakes to watch the business interests of farmers in legislation, and in agricultural politics generally. Originally the principal impulse was probably the need for safeguarding agricultural interests in the rationing days during the war and the Revolution; since then, however, its attention has moved to taxation, business politics, subsidies, etc. While, therefore, not simply or exactly a co-operative organisation, the promotion of co-operative enterprise finds prominent place in its programme, and its active solicitude and labours have resulted in many new consumer co-operatives, co-operative creameries, forest preservation societies, cattle trade associations, etc.

The Union has also played an important part in the formation of several business federations, and, moreover, organises trade in agricultural produce in the interests of the farmers. Weekly quotation lists and market reports are sent out, freights and railway rates are watched and questioned, and export of agricultural produce is encouraged and facilitated. The latest figures show 309 local societies with some 18,500 members in 16 district associations. Two newspapers *Maaseudun Tulevaisuus* (*The Future of the Countryside*) and *Maataloustuottaja* (*The Agricultural Producer*) command circulations of 25,000 and 5,000 respectively, representing thus a considerable influence upon popular opinion.

To this Union belong all classes of farmers; of its membership 17 per cent. are smallholders, 40 per cent. hold small to medium acreage, 28 per cent. medium, 12 per cent. over medium, and 3 per cent. large farms. Naturally, that this general association of farming interests keenly appreciates the value of co-operation, and collaborates so effectively in its practical promotion, is of high significance and service to the co-operative movement. A similar appreciation of the benefits of co-operation is shown by the increasingly important special associations of smallholders, active principally in the areas where cottars formerly thirled have won their independence, and by the two Central Unions of Agricultural Societies, Swedish-speaking and Finnish respectively.

CHAPTER III

CONSUMERS' CO-OPERATION TO 1917

TAMMERFORS MEETING, 1903: A CENTRAL ORGANISATION FORMED FOR CONSUMER CO-OPERATIVES

The example set by Tammerfors proved extremely fruitful in the early years of the century. Consumer co-operatives found, naturally, earlier acceptance in towns and industrial communities, but soon enough they began to be a common feature of rural areas as well. Probably the first country society was started in 1900 in S. Österbotten. By 1903 that had twenty successors, and recruiting continued strong. Pellervo's educational work was conspicuous in these early stages, and the need for association to improve conditions of living was clamant among all classes. Industrial workers, cottars, smallholders, teachers, railwaymen, all felt the pinch and the lack of that independence that only freedom from the shackles of debt assures.

As yet the various societies did not combine in any way. Each purchased from private wholesalers, to whom, sooner or later, they became credit-tied. Capital was inadequate, as can be understood, and management left much to be desired. Lacking central organisation, systematic educational work too was heavily handicapped.

The initiative to closer collaboration came also from Finland's co-operative Rochdale—Tammerfors. The executives of the local societies convened a meeting there of all Finnish co-operatives on May 31, 1903, for the purpose of appointing a propaganda agent, to act also as consultant, and to manage a central office. But the question of co-operative wholesaling intruded irresistibly on the meeting and provided the main topic of discussion. Three different proposals emerged, including one from Pellervo. Finally a committee was appointed to investigate and report.

The following year this committee submitted a proposal to establish a Central Wholesale Society to explore and prepare the way, and to assist in building up Finnish co-operation on sound co-operative and business principles. After full examination this was adopted, with the proviso that the new Central should proceed to actual trading as soon as opportunity offered. Of the 37 societies represented at the meeting, 12 affiliated at once, including the three Tammerfors societies. Among those taking part in the meeting was Väinö Tanner, then a co-operative manager in Åbo, later Prime Minister of the Republic, and now President of the International Co-operative Alliance.

A management committee and an executive were appointed, and a name was bestowed: S.O.K. Besides encouraging new societies and keeping existing societies safe and sound, the officials of S.O.K. saw to it that Pellervo model rules were accepted wherever possible, that credit sale was prohibited, that compulsory shares were fixed at 10 to 25 marks (8s. to £1), and that further liability did not in any case exceed £4 per member — societies were generally constituted on limited members' liability—and that no society was formed until 75 to 100 persons had undertaken to subscribe share capital.

Besides expounding the importance of co-operative activity and co-operative principles the consultant had to canvas for affiliation to S.O.K., and secure circulation and reading for co-operative literature. The general Press began to take notice of co-operation at work, and from 1905 a special co-operative newspaper was issued by S.O.K.: *Yhteishyvä*, still running, and, since 1909, accompanied by a Swedish edition: *Samarbete*.

The ultimate aim of wholesaling was always kept

in view, and was actually realised in the early summer of 1905. There arose thus a central organisation of dual function, combining trading, education, and propaganda, on the Swiss pattern. At the first annual meeting of S.O.K. in 1905 alterations were made in the rules to facilitate the affiliation of the South-West Finland Co-operative Union, a purchase federation, and its newspaper, subsequently merged in *Yhteishyvä*.

Consumer co-operatives in Finland had thus been brought within one fold. In 1905 the Hankkija Wholesale Society also began operations as an extension and reorganisation of the Pellervo Agency, started in 1901 for the purchase of agricultural requirements by farmers through their consumer co-operatives direct from manufacturers or private wholesalers. This new departure necessitated a division of labour between S.O.K. and Hankkija, so agreement was made that S.O.K. should cease handling agricultural requisites and feeding stuffs, while Hankkija was to refrain from trading in consumption goods.

First Decade: Rapid Development of S.O.K. Movement

S.O.K.'s first year's sales exceeded £40,000, and rapid expansion followed. Consumer co-operation had definitely won a footing in town and country. About this time S.O.K.'s educational efforts were powerfully seconded by the grant of the universal franchise with its consequent stimulus to enquiry and responsibility. The following table shows very remarkable increase of membership between 1905 and 1910. Affiliation to S.O.K. increased correspondingly, societies becoming shareholders that had so far contented themselves with buying only. Much room for improvement existed here; of 123 societies purchasing in 1905 only 27 were shareholders.

By 1908 societies' sales had reached £570,000, and 115 societies were affiliated, nearly one-fourth of the whole. A rationalisation effected in 1909–10, weeding out failures and amalgamating others, for a time reduced sales. The number of local societies fell from 512 in 1910 to 415 in 1914. Nevertheless, from 1912 membership of S.O.K. again moved swiftly upwards, partly a mustering of forces in the domestic quarrel that was proceeding, and of which later—until in 1916, just before the storm broke—89 per cent. of the possible was reached. Sales had kept pace, and increased substantially, allowing even for the intervening fall in the mark.

The rapid progress of these years is well shown in the table appended:

Year.	Number of Societies.	Number of Shops.	Membership.	Total Sales.	Purchased from S.O.K.
				£	£
1903	72	—	14,000	200,000	—
1905	155	210	26,000	440,000	40,000
1910	405	695	79,000	1,760,000	560,000
1913	378	755	82,000	2,240,000	920,000
1915	413	980	111,000	3,480,000	1,400,000
1916	—	—	182,000	—	2,880,000

Policy Disputes

For some time, however, there had been growing dissension despite the splendid development. There was no disagreement on basic principles, co-operative or business. Different views were held of the relation of consumers' co-operation to other movements for political and social reform. All along, Finnish co-operation, wholesale and retail, had rigidly adhered to neutrality in politics, in religion, in language, had insisted on free and open membership, and had gathered adherents from all classes. No faction thought seriously to disturb this neutrality. Certainly one small group advocated closer union with and financial support of the Labour Party, on Belgian lines, but this group commanded little attention or following.

Further contention arose concerning the attitude of S.O.K. and its societies to and treatment of employees, on the movement's connection with producer co-operatives and on many minor questions. On the other hand, there was no division along lines of language. The resultant disputes were really few and inessential; mainly they concerned whether societies should conclude collective agreements with their staffs—local production had now attained considerable dimensions—whether only Trade Union members should be employed, whether societies should concede Trade Union demands for boycott of goods in their quarrels, etc. The relations between consumer co-operatives and the farmer movement led to further words, which came to a head with a proposal that Pellervo should be reorganised into a super-organisation for the whole Co-operative Movement.

Reform of the S.O.K. itself was also pressed. Separate organisations, on German or British lines, for trading and for education and propaganda, had been urged from the beginning. Partly to meet this continuing demand, for which quite a good case was made out, a General Co-operative Union, Yleinen Osuuskauppojen Liitto or Y.O.L., was formed as a complement to but still subordinate to S.O.K., with district organisation, directing education, propaganda, etc., locally in co-operation with S.O.K. via Y.O.L. The latter was to convene an Annual Congress, almost its only direct function, for the discussion of educational and propaganda methods and furtherance. From many quarters, and especially from the town societies, came still an insistent demand for Y.O.L.'s complete independence.

The Question of Representation Becomes Acute

These themes kept Congress busy. At length a settlement, completely satisfactory to both parties, appeared in sight, when another and more serious disagreement arose. At the formation of S.O.K. there was no great difference in the size of the constituent societies. All were about equally small and weak, and little attention or objection was therefore aroused when the rules of S.O.K., in accordance with the Act, allowed to each society, irrespective of size, one delegate only in General Meeting and one vote. In time, as societies in populous centres grew rapidly in membership, this was felt to be an injustice, and repeated proposals were submitted for alterations in this respect, so that large societies might have more representation.

Determined opposition was offered by the small societies, and the proposal was always lost. Overtures to the opponents of change were fruitless. The annual battle on this topic aggravated other differences, which then assumed importance not warranted by the real circumstances, since the activities in general of all the societies remained in complete harmony with basic co-operative principles. For example, there was no attempt whatever to divert surplus from its proper function in the society's service, to distribute the final balance among the members in any other way than in proportion to purchases, or to restrict membership.

Secession

The situation became more and more untenable, until in 1916 a number of societies withdrew from Y.O.L., and founded, November 1916, a new Union, K.K. (Kulutusosuuskuntien Keskusliitto), with voting rights proportional to membership, so soon as the Act should be amended. These societies still continued to purchase from S.O.K., until the 1917 Congress rejected their proposal to convert S.O.K. into a joint-stock company in order to allow proportional representation under the law. Thereupon the K.K. societies set up their own wholesale OTK (Osuustukkukauppa) in December 1917. Societies purchasing therefrom were at once expelled from S.O.K., and the rift in Finnish consumer co-operation became definite and final. While the larger number of societies remained loyal to S.O.K. and Y.O.L., the membership that deserted to K.K. and OTK was quite half of the total.

The Character of the Movement Unchanged

A foreigner, strange to the procession of contributory developments and to the shifting environment, naturally refrains from any attempt to cast the blame for this partition. Quite incontrovertibly, however, it may be asserted that there was no serious difference in the conception of the character and objects of co-operative effort. After the separation both parties persisted on true consumer co-operative lines; both have affiliated to the International Co-operative Alliance, they frequently act together when consumer co-operative interests are threatened, and in 1928 both joined in membership of the Scandinavian Wholesale Society.

Nor can the secession be attributed to party politics, for in each of the diverging streams political tendencies were similarly mingled, and neither has shown any inclination to support any political party, to promote parliamentary candidatures, or to favour factional interests in any way involving infringement of the cardinal principle of political neutrality. Even if, broadly, the political sympathies of the majority of the members in the two movements may possibly be said to favour opposite camps, no harmful influence has ever resulted on their zeal for co-operative expansion and the realisation of its aims. True, during the disturbed years before and after 1918 and its Civil War, the working classes preferred the younger movement and the conservatively minded the other, but that is easily explainable from the bitter antagonisms then rampant. On the other hand, never has the programme of either been tainted by any suggestion of class aversion to the detriment of or in conflict with co-operation. And that is the main thing.

Scrutiny of membership reveals S.O.K. as predominantly a farming class consumers' co-operation; K.K. as mainly supported by townspeople and industrial workers. This distinction has not arisen from any difference in needs requiring satisfaction; a number of typical town societies still belong to the former: Varuboden and Helsingin Osuuskauppa in Helsingfors, Tuotanto in Tammerfors, Osuusliike Torkkeli in Viborg, and several others, while the latter could always claim a considerable element of smallholders, cottars, and farmworkers all over the country. The division into "town" and "country" types is rather attributable to the rules dispute, and its rupture between large and small societies, the former naturally preponderating in towns and other industrial centres.

The interval is yet too short to allow opinion on the effects of this separation on the development of consumer co-operation in Finland. Since 1917 there has been rapid expansion of co-operative activity, membership and turnover have increased very similarly in both, and there is distinct tendency generally to ascribe this, if not entirely, yet very largely, to the competition of the two, or rather to their emulation in lauding the advantages of co-operation among the various classes, and in seeking to convert ever more and more, not merely into customers of co-operative stores, but interested members of societies.

On the other hand, the division of the movement

into two sections in so small a national household as Finland would seem in the long run sure to prove an obstacle to the full development of its powers, especially as regards production and capital resources. In the last decade both have certainly advanced remarkably in production, but co-ordination has been lacking, and direction has been faulty, with the result that productive ventures, instead of complementing each other, have been coincident and quite unnecessarily duplicate.

Recently, however, a growing desire finds expression for some form of understanding to operate production in undertakings so dimensioned as to enable their output to compete effectively with the rationalised and amalgamated production of to-day. The project certainly presents great practical difficulties, but its realisation must soon become a necessity.

Especially where monopoly is to be coerced back into methods and prices less inimical to consumers, by setting up competing enterprises in the interests of the latter, is a thorough co-ordination of co-operatively organised consumers' purchasing and capital power throughout the whole nation a necessary preliminary to success. The well-wisher must hope that perception of this will gradually ripen into full appreciation with a united front where that is needed. The common membership of the Scandinavian Wholesale indicates movement in this direction, and in time all must realise that the best results can only be expected from united, not from divided, action.

CHAPTER IV

THE DEVELOPMENT OF THE "NEUTRAL" MOVEMENT —S.O.K.—AND ITS SOCIETIES AFTER 1917

From the beginning of 1917 only societies affiliated to S.O.K. were allowed to purchase therefrom. So over one hundred rejoined. Thus was made good again the loss of those expelled as already described.

S.O.K. Societies, 1918–1928

Year.	Number of Societies.	Their Membership.	Number of Shops.	Sales, in £1,000.
1918	434	128,053	988	7,800
1919	477	161,027	1,351	3,450
1920	484	174,570	1,587	6,000
1921	482	178,072	1,724	5,150
1922	466	174,520	1,694	5,150
1923	462	172,938	1,673	5,600
1924	459	178,997	1,700	6,250
1925	451	181,892	1,749	6,700
1926	434	187,982	1,817	7,200
1927	423	197,182	1,903	8,300
1928	419	207,707	2,004	9,500
1929	425	217,170	2,128	9,700

The troubled years immediately succeeding, accompanied as they were by economic unheavals of devastating character, were of course not without influence on the development of consumer co-operation. Both movements were seriously affected by the Civil War and its consequences, although figures show K.K. societies as suffering most. Violent quarrels in societies, in echo of the political strife then raging, caused a number to leave K.K. and reaffiliate to S.O.K., which, with the spur of these disastrous times contributing, substantially increased its membership, and even more its turnover, as appears from the table following. Allowing for the reduced value of the mark, there was still real increase of sales. From 1920 to 1923 improvement flagged, until stabilisation of the currency was effected. Then upward movement was resumed, and has continued steadily since.

Systematic Amalgamation

The number of societies has diminished year by year since 1920, the result of deliberate concentration campaigns carried on ever since the war, actuated by firm conviction that only so can the strongest, most efficient, and most serviceable societies be built up. The creation of a new society is as far as possible avoided if a consumer co-operative exists in the neighbourhood capable of serving the area. Difficulties are met, naturally, in a country where population is so sparse. Frequently, therefore, regional societies are formed to supply several parishes from some suitable centre of communications. The largest of these attached to S.O.K. is Keski-Pohjanmaan Osuuskauppa with 4,275 members, 30 shops, and sales of £210,000 in the year. For comparison may be mentioned that the S.O.K. society with the greatest membership, Varuboden, in Helsingfors, has just under 5,000 members. On the average S.O.K. societies in 1927 had 466 members each and 4·6 shops—excellent figures in the circumstances.

Amalgamation has made possible vast improvement in shops and equipment, most notably, of course, in the town societies. But even in remoter tracts are to be found shops that bear comparison with those of much wealthier countries of far longer co-operative history.

The growth in membership and in the network of shops has encouraged a remarkable diversity of trade. Not only grocery and provisions are sold, but also cloth and knitting wools, shoes, household utensils, dungarees, to some extent outfitting and dress goods, also special farming lines such as agricultural machinery, artificial manures, feeding stuffs, oils, cement, ropes, canvas, and general ironmongery. Country stores often carry also seeds, gardening requirements, brushes, dairy plant, and other necessities including chemicals, salt, crystal soda, henfeed and poultry appliances, barbed wire, fishing requirements, hunting kit, explosives, cycles, even motor-cycles, motor-cars, and tractors—goods many of which are rarely found in the consumer co-operative stores of other countries.

Sale of Members' Farm Produce

A highly important trade is done in an opposite direction, i.e. the sale to members of produce bought from other members: grain, hay, eggs, farm butter, meat, garden produce. Some of the larger country societies, especially in South and West Finland, have thus erected corn silos, quite modern if unpretentious, for gathering and storing the grain that members intend for sale, there to be cleaned, treated, and kept for the market. This is a development that grows apace, every encouragement being given by S.O.K. to the direct sale of members' produce for consumption.

Of the total sales by societies in 1921, close on £4,400,000 consisted of goods for consumption sold direct to the consumer, and £880,000 of agricultural requirements, including agricultural produce. (The statistics do not distinguish here.) In 1927 the figures were £6,000,000 and £2,260,000 respectively, i.e. the latter group accounted for not less than 27·2 per cent. of the whole turnover. And finality is far from reached, for of the total membership a good two-thirds, or 67·9 per cent., own or occupy land, while 19·5 per cent. are salaried officials—teachers, municipal workers, railwaymen, private employees, etc.

—12·1 per cent. industrial workers, and 5 per cent. collective members: societies, companies, local authorities, schools, etc.

Low Dividends; Small Shares

The consumer co-operatives of both wings in Finland pursue the same policy of keeping down prices and refund or dividend, practically dictating prices where they operate, and especially diminishing the working expenses of agriculture. Most are satisfied with 1 to 2 per cent. of dividend. The average net surplus of S.O.K. societies for 1927 was 2·1 per cent. on sales, but was formerly much lower even—in 1921–2, 1·2 per cent. Obviously such dividend is a minor consideration. After the war-time and post-war inflation of prices, when the capital and reserves of societies lost 80 to 90 per cent. of their value, every effort has had to be strained to strengthen capital resources. So, on an average, 70 to 75 per cent. of the available surplus is transferred to reserve.

This funding is so much the more necessary in that Finnish consumer co-operatives, of both categories, work with a very modest share contribution. Pellervo's model rules prescribed members' share subscription at 8s. to £1, which, at the beginning of the century, having regard to the meagre incomes obtaining and the scarcity of ready money in peasant households, was the maximum considered possible. When stabilisation had finally reduced the real value of the mark by seven-eighths, the aforementioned Clause 19 of the Act proved a serious obstacle to financial improvement. The modification introduced in 1927 has not yet had time to take much effect. In S.O.K. societies the average share capital per member subscribed is thus only about 2s. 3d. To-day, when new societies are formed, by amalgamation or otherwise, the share capital stipulated for membership is seldom less than 10s., still a paltry figure.

Finance Difficulties

In consequence of the economic difficulties that have harassed the country, societies have been obliged to resort to borrowed capital to a far greater extent than, for example, in more fortunate Sweden. Against the total assets of S.O.K. societies in 1927 only 27·4 per cent. was opposed by share capital and reserves, but the proportion has steadily risen from 20·8 per cent. in 1921.

The borrowed capital is not, however, of a character that tends to undermine the independence of societies, since it consists very largely of the deposited savings of the members, loans from members, and advances from credit institutions of kindred character, such as Co-operative Credit Banks and other Savings Banks. In addition, the advances are usually for long terms.

The first savings departments in S.O.K. societies were opened in 1917; there are now 170. In all, the deposits therein, and loans from members, are together equal to 34·2 per cent. of the liabilities. Loans from ordinary banks, Co-operative Credit Banks, and other Savings Banks amount to £706,000, or 24·5 per cent. of total liabilities.

Here, however, should be mentioned that societies' buildings and sites stand in the balance-sheets at their old figures, so that considerable concealed reserves exist. Mortgages are generally taken only for new buildings. In 1927 they amounted to £75,000.

No Credit

Quite remarkably, considering that most of the members are farmers and much of the trade is done in farming requirements, credit is allowed by few of the societies. Of the combined assets in 1927 only £171,000, equal to 2·1 per cent. of turnover, was represented by individual credit, and less than £42,000, or 0·5 per cent., by group credit. The trading or working credit that farmers require is, therefore, not supplied to any extent by consumer co-operatives. This refusal of credit has been strictly enforced on grounds of principle since the very commencement. Any necessary credit is procured, and very largely as personal credit, from Co-operative Credit Banks and Savings Banks. What these have meant, especially to the poorer farmers and cottars, is discussed in the chapter on Co-operative Credit Banks.

Still the capital problem is undeniably the most pressing. Not only is more varied range of stock necessary, but shops must be modernised and new premises erected to keep up with the times, and the need for productive undertakings grows ever more clamant. Of these, societies in 1927 had 74; including 48 bakeries, 11 tanneries, and 3 aerated-water factories, with few exceptions small, and their total output only £155,000. Co-operators in Finland are, however, thoroughly seized of the necessity to avoid risking the independence of societies, and rather concentrate on strengthening their finances, waiting and delaying productive development so as to maintain a sound relation between the needs of the members and the scarcity of available accumulated capital.

S.O.K. Sales doubled in Ten Years

The development of the Wholesale Society since 1917 has kept pace with that of the societies. Sales rose from £2,650,000 in 1918 to £5,200,000 in 1928, and £5,450,000 in 1929. The services S.O.K. has been able to offer societies have continuously increased, and to-day there are comparatively few commodities retailed by them that S.O.K. does not supply. Agricultural requisites are obtained, as mentioned already, from Hankkija and Labor.

Just as S.O.K. has extended its scope and facilities, has the percentage of societies' purchases therefrom increased. In 1921 the percentage of sales by S.O.K. societies representing purchases from their wholesale society was 37·9, and rose by 1928 to 76·3. Loyalty is thus very keen, in turn a proof of the steadily increased advantages a wholesale brings in proportion as the movement expands.

S.O.K. business is sectionalised into (1) Grocery, (2) Provision and Meats, (3) Drapery and Hardware, and (4) Office Supplies, and by means of a net of sales offices and warehouses all over the country, with excellent display and storage, distribution of commodities to societies proceeds rapidly, systematically, economically. The Helsingfors office is housed in the main central premises, a stately turreted building across the street from Eliel Saarinen's famous architectural masterpiece—the Central Railway Station.

Depots have been established in Viborg, Uleåborg, Tammerfors, Vasa, Jyväskylä, Kuopio, Åbo, Kotka, and Gamlakarleby, all housed in S.O.K.'s own buildings, and warehouses are provided in Mariehamn, Raumo, and Björneborg. These well-stocked branch establishments give local societies every facility and choice, and have dispensed with much of the need for commercial travellers.

S.O.K. Production

Wholesale production began as early as 1914, but was long sorely handicapped by want of capital. In that year a brush factory, a dressmaking department, a fruit and spice packing warehouse, and a coffee-roasting house were begun in Helsingfors. In 1916 a chicory factory was added. For these purposes a large building was acquired in the town, but this was commandeered by the Russian military, and was not again available until 1918. The factory, considerably modernised and enlarged, is now one of the two main centres of production and accommodation, with an assembling shop for cycle building, a repair establishment for typewriters, etc., and a knitting factory.

In 1914 (when contracted supplies were refused because of the World War) a small match factory was bought in Kolho. This was burned down in 1916, and later a new factory was erected at Vaajakoski, an eminently suitable traffic centre near Jyväskylä, with abundance of the necessary poplar timber in the vicinity. The new factory is a model of modern efficiency and organisation.

At this ideally situated Vaajakoski, S.O.K. is gradually creating an industrial community of quite unique character. Much of the surrounding land now belongs to S.O.K., and its rivers provide ample water force for conversion into electric power sufficient to meet all possible needs of the whole community. Besides the match factory, not one of the largest, but producing 60,000 cases in the year, there have been erected a margarine factory, completed in 1928, to which have now been removed the manufacture also of sweets and confections, a saw-mill, a woodwork factory, a box factory, a brush factory—transferred from Helsingfors—a fruit essence factory, and a flour-mill for local needs, all very modern and efficient.

Houses have been erected for the workers, and the settlement is entirely co-operative. Until recently S.O.K. owned few productive enterprises outside Vaajakoski—a macaroni factory in Viborg, an up-to-date brickworks in Jämsä, and a herring saltery in Sastmola. In 1928 work was begun on a flour-mill in

Uleåborg, which was finished and taken into use in autumn, 1929. This, the first large co-operative flour-mill in Finland, has an annual output capacity of 12,000 tons. At present only rye and oats are milled, but other grain will be added as required.

The total value of S.O.K.'s own manufactures for 1928 was £414,000, about 8 per cent. of its total sales, not an imposing figure certainly, but very creditable in face of the difficulties encountered. For some years, for example, the Swedish Match Trust fought fiercely to capture the market of S.O.K.'s match factory. Agreement has now, however, been reached with the Trust under which a considerable influence on price fixing has been conceded. The home price cannot be raised except with the consent of two Co-operative Wholesales, S.O.K. and OTK, the latter also manufacturing matches in Tammerfors. On the other hand, sale for export, under the same agreement, is subject to regulation by the whole Finnish match production acting jointly.

Uleåborg flour-mill, when fully utilised, will of course considerably increase the proportion of production to sales.

S.O.K.: Advisory and Propaganda Activity

Besides its trading activities and their auxiliaries a number of other departments are accommodated in S.O.K.'s headquarters, of which may be mentioned the credit department, the legal department, the works or building department, and the laboratory. Once a month societies send in to S.O.K. a balance statement. Thus the credit department is able to follow their development and tender advice for future guidance, especially as to building extension, in which the works department and its architects render valuable assistance.

The credit department also controls the auditors, who operate both centrally and locally, and the benefit of whose responsible work can scarcely be over-estimated. They supervise the book-keeping of societies and officially audit their accounts, advise in business management, and are available always for consultation generally. The laboratory tests samples for the sale departments, helping thus to exercise close control over the nation's food supplies. The legal department advises in matters of law, and the works department designs shops and equipment.

Educational and propaganda work is assigned to the Advisory Bureau, which at the same time administers for the Central Union: Y.O.L. Hence issue newspapers: *Yhteishyvä*, in Finnish, with 155,000 weekly circulation; *Samarbete*, in Swedish (24,500), obviously popular organs among the 347 Finnish-speaking, 75 Swedish, and 2 bilingual societies, and their 208,000 members; also the more technical magazine for management officials and employees: *Osuuskauppalehti*, Finnish (5,500), and *Handelslaget*, Swedish (1,000).

Other publications include an annual diary in 70,000 to 80,000 copies, a number of occasional pamphlets and books, rules and account forms, and the S.O.K. year book, with statistics and reports of the year's trade. Lectures and propaganda are also arranged by S.O.K., which, like neighbouring countries and like its colleague K.K., has pressed the film into common and successful service.

Supervision of societies' Savings Banks, and a large measure of the relevant book-keeping, falls to the same bureau. Finnish law imposes State control on all banking, but the State is satisfied to entrust its functions as regards societies affiliated to S.O.K. to that body, which has set up a special staff for the purpose.

S.O.K. runs an employment agency, found helpful by societies with positions to fill, and further arranges one- and two-day classes for staffs in rural areas. About 130 such classes have been held in the last five years.

S.O.K.'s Co-operative College

Staff training is undertaken by the Wholesale's Commercial College—"Finland's Co-operative Business College"—in Helsingfors, working in two sections: a Finnish and a Swedish-speaking. General commercial education is supplied such as fits the pupils to become branch managers in retail societies, and eventually general managers. Pupils are received every second year in the Swedish division, the course lasting two years. Thus there are always three classes running: a first- and second-year Finnish, and a first- or second-year Swedish. A thorough training is given, and is supplemented by special courses for actual branch managers, for book-keepers, and for certain special positions.

Summer schools have also been introduced, in various districts, in Finnish or Swedish, as appropriate. Lectures on co-operation and general economics alternate with amusement and recreation. The Swedish schools are held usually in Österbotten, in the Åland Islands, or in South Finland, the Finnish in different areas, but always amid scenes of natural beauty and popular interest. Excursions, bathing, lazing take turn with serious study, and the evenings are merry with the old singing games and folk-dances.

S.O.K. Organisation and Government

The organisation of S.O.K. presents several peculiar features. The supreme authority is the Annual General Meeting, which is held at the same time as the Y.O.L. Congress. The latter deals only with matters of general importance, while all elections, etc., take place at the

S.O.K. meeting. There the Supervisory Council of eighteen is elected, the accounts are discussed and approved along with the management report, and business of major importance is debated and decided.

While each society has one vote only, it may send several delegates—all but one voteless. One-third of the Supervisory Council retire each year. The Council, when elected, appoints the Managing Executive and the more important officials—departmental heads, district managers, secretary, etc. The Executive's minutes are submitted to the Supervisory Council, which also has initiative rights; but any resolutions or proposals issuing therefrom must be timely tabled so that the Executive may have time to investigate what is involved. Current management falls entirely to the Executive, but the Supervisory Council decide such questions as the commencement of new branches of production, larger building outlay, purchase of property, etc.

Of recent years district organisation has increased largely in importance. Societies pay a certain annual subscription in their districts, commonly 1¼d. a member, to provide funds for local propaganda, arranged in conjunction with S.O.K.'s Advisory Bureau. District meetings are held in the autumn, when the district executives, each of three members, with three deputies or substitutes, are appointed.

During the year, meetings of these executives are held with committee members and local society managers to discuss the co-operative affairs of the district, to devise ways and means of consolidating finance—most necessary!—and for the discovery and application of better business methods. Once a year the Supervisory Council meets all the District Executives. These gatherings are especially profitable in that the position and possibilities of societies and districts are thoroughly explored, and contact is maintained between headquarters and the outposts and over the whole terrain. An annual meeting of general managers, two from each district, is similarly convened for like purpose.

The Capital Problem

The position and authority of S.O.K. have thus in the course of years in more than one respect become solidly established, but certainly not without grave difficulties, especially in connection with post-war stabilisation. Inflation stole the bulk of capital and reserves. In 1918 these amounted to £300,000; now they total £480,000. By rule three-fourths of any surplus is to be allocated to reserve, which for 1928 meant an accretion thereto of £72,000.

The share capital subscribed by the societies in membership is of much less consequence, amounting to little over £4,000, or only some decimal fraction per cent. of turnover. S.O.K. has, therefore, to enlist the aid of borrowed capital. On December 31, 1928, long-term loans outstanding amounted to £145,000, short-term loans to £600,000, in a liability total of £1,260,000. But again, buildings, sites, and productive establishments appear in the balance-sheet at original figures, less depreciation, and therefore represent much more real value than is indicated.

CHAPTER V

THE "PROGRESSIVE" CONSUMER CO-OPERATIVE MOVEMENT AND ITS CENTRAL ORGANISATIONS

When, in 1918, the rupture became final, the seceders, K.K. and OTK, called themselves the "Progressive Co-operative Movement"; the others assumed the title "Neutral Co-operative Movement". The new section made rapid progress, impeded for a time by the injury inflicted by the Civil War, when, as already told, a number of societies returned to the S.O.K. fold. In part these soon came back to K.K. Before then, and until dual membership was vetoed, a large number of K.K. societies had belonged to both camps.

Much the same amalgamation influence is traceable in the figures appended for K.K. societies, which have pursued a policy similar to those attached to S.O.K. They have found, as in other countries, that membership and turnover increase most rapidly in the larger societies. While the number of societies is seen to remain

DEVELOPMENT OF K.K. SOCIETIES SINCE 1917.

Year.	Number of Societies.	Their Membership.	Number of Shops.	Sales, in £1,000.
1917	166	132,000	757	8,140
1918	87	95,000	503	3,730
1919	94	120,000	611	3,970
1920	106	144,000	744	4,800
1921	116	158,000	859	3,340
1922	113	161,000	898	3,550
1923	113	173,000	957	4,890
1924	110	185,000	1,044	5,530
1925	113	197,000	1,126	5,780
1926	113	208,000	1,176	5,950
1927	112	214,000	1,295	6,250
1928	112	226,000	1,346	7,030
1929	112	239,000	1,452	—

stationary the membership continually advances. Each member represents in general a household, although in some societies endeavour is made to persuade every adult to join and take live interest in the movement to the extent of subscribing capital or investing savings for its use. Development since 1917 is shown by the figures in the table on page 63.

An Average of 2,000 Members and £60,000 Annual Sales

K.K. societies are thus on the average much bigger than those affiliated to S.O.K. Not only the town societies operate on a large scale, but many of the rural as well, organised as regional where settlement and communications favour. The average is inflated by the comparative hugeness of several of the largest societies, among them Elanto in Helsingfors with 41,000 members and £1,700,000 annual turnover.

This average size grows uninterruptedly. Of the whole, only three have annual sales of less than £5,200, 52 range from that to £26,000, 28 from £26,000 to £52,000, 14 from £52,000 to £104,000, and 15 exceed the latter sum. The number of shops per society moves in sympathy; 13 now against 6 in 1918: 18 have more than 20 each. The largest are Elanto, already mentioned; Voima in Tammerfors, with 13,000 members and £389,000 sales; Viborg with 11,000 members and £362,000 turnover; Uleåborg, 11,000 and £346,000; Kotka, Jyväskylä, Björneborg, St. Michel, Vasa, Ruokolahti (Imatra), etc. Several of these trade far beyond the town in which their headquarters lie: thus Elanto serves 11 outside parishes, Voima, in Tammerfors, 10, Björneborg 11, Uleåborg 15, Viborg 9, St. Michel 8, etc.

Which shows again how inaccurate would be any description of K.K. as exclusively an urban movement.

1929 analysis gives 69,000 members, or 28·6 per cent., as farmers or farm workers. Of the remainder, 7,000 or 2·8 per cent. were officials of various kinds, 20,000 or 8·3 per cent. clerks, etc., 111,000 or 46·5 per cent. industrial and municipal workers, 19,000 or 8·1 per cent. other workers, while 2,600 or 1·1 per cent. were group members, and 6,000 or 2·7 per cent. of unknown occupation. The remaining 1·9 per cent. belonged to the professions.

Representative Government in K.K. Societies

The growing size of K.K. societies soon made resort necessary to a representative system of government. The open Annual General Meeting, which every member may attend, if a meeting-place large enough can be found, remains only in the small societies; in the larger this has been superseded by a Delegate Meeting of from 30 to 60 representatives. At present about one-third of the K.K. societies have this form of government. In its main features the system agrees with that generally obtaining in Continental Europe, except that proportional representation is operated.

For election purposes the members may group themselves as they please. Usually they muster along party political lines: yet very rarely have political differences found their way into the committee room. Once elected, the representatives vie in serving the societies' real interests, and adopt purely co-operative points of view in their work, finding probably hopeless any design they may have cherished of converting the heretics on the Board to their own political faith. In times of excitement much irrelevancy may mark the unavoidable discussion accompanying the elections; but, on the other hand, the block voting system has been considered to increase interest in and for the society. The percentage voting in Elanto, for example, 20 to 50, seems to corroborate.

The Delegate Assembly proceeds, after election, to appoint the Supervisory Council, which in turn appoints a Managing Executive of 3 to 5. The Managing Director is, by rule and by virtue of his office, President of the Executive, which may include others of the permanent staff. The largest societies, to the number of 40, have adopted this form of government. In the medium-sized, 38 in number, the Annual General Meeting elects the Supervisory Council, and the latter appoints the Managing Executive. The smaller societies, 34, elect their Management Executives directly in the Annual General Meeting. The first two groups follow K.K. model rules, the other Pellervo's.

All the larger societies have also Shop Committees, which, on the one hand, supervise the shops in the interests of the members, and, on the other, arrange meetings, soirées, etc., at which the general business of the societies is discussed, resolutions are considered and forwarded, and co-operative educational work prosecuted.

8,000 Different Articles on Sale: Co-operative Restaurants

The trade of K.K. societies is very motley and varied. The large regional societies, serving both town and country, sell practically everything: in special shops grocery, bread, meat, milk, and often drapery and shoes; soap, perfumes, toilet articles, drugs, household utensils, ironmongery, building material, machinery, tools and implements, seed, grain, feeding stuffs, artificial manures. In large societies 7,000 to 8,000 different lines may be carried, and still the number grows.

Café and restaurant trade has already been noted as a special co-operative feature in Finland. This applies even more to K.K. societies than to S.O.K. Scarcely one of the larger co-operatives but has its "ravintola"

(Finnish for "restaurant"), often exceedingly attractive, with music, wireless, flowers, and artistic decoration on ceiling and walls—a recreation and gathering centre for the whole town or community. Prohibition, which is law in Finland, is rigidly enforced, and the better class of people prefer the co-operative restaurant. Dividend is paid on restaurant payments, and although, like the shops, they are open to all and sundry, their co-operative character is never in doubt. About one-fifth of the total sales of societies are calculated to be made to non-members, but even these, if they join up, are credited full dividend on what purchases they have made.

In 1929 there were 94 cafés and restaurants belonging to K.K. societies, of which Elanto possessed 12.

Local Production: Shop Improvement

K.K. societies have made notable progress in production; 72, no less, have bakeries, dairies, aerated-water and soft-drink factories, tailoring workrooms, boot-repairing shops, woodworking and carpentry factories, prepared-meat factories, the last-named not so numerous. Quite commonly one society has four or five of these—for example, a bakery, an aerated-water works, a flour-mill, a meat factory, boot-repair shop, etc.

The smallest of the "Big Five", Kotka, in the Kymmene valley, has all these, and then a timber yard, a saw-mill, a metal workshop, a butchery, and a farm on which pigs are bred and fed. In all, the 72 societies own 161 productive undertakings with 1,452 workers, and a combined output of £1,560,000, equal to 21·8 per cent. of total sales. In 1918 societies' own manufactures amounted to £540,000, or 14·57 per cent. of sales. Since then the number of undertakings has multiplied threefold.

The co-operative baking industry in particular takes high rank in Finland, leading the way in the use of modern machinery. Elanto's great bakery in Helsingfors, the largest and probably the finest in the North, has served as an example avidly followed by Tammerfors, Uleåborg, Kotka, and other societies. These hygienic, generously lighted, and highly scientific bakeries have proved excellent advertisement and pull for the co-operative movement. S.O.K. societies have also some excellent bakeries, as, for example, Tuotanto in Tammerfors. Bread prices run low in Finland, due undoubtedly to this powerful co-operative influence.

Shops and stores reach a very high standard, too. Foreign co-operators know Elanto shops very well, and cite them often, with every justification, as models; both aesthetically and hygienically they take foremost rank. Other societies, principally of course the larger, are little if any behind; not only in Helsingfors are pleasant, comfortable, well-adapted grocery shops, meat shops with splendid cold storage, dairy shops in dainty colouring, and special shops of the highest class to be found; in Tammerfors, Viborg, Vasa, to name at random a few centres visited, the author found the same high standards obtaining. Voima's newest premises in Tammerfors are the last note in this perfection. To this end K.K.'s works department and architects are invaluable in the assistance they render.

The Capital Problem; Shares; Savings

This commendably high level of shop equipment and the excellent standard of productive establishments are the more remarkable since capital has been so difficult to raise in the K.K. movement. Share subscription is very small there, too. Indeed, share capital plays scarcely any part in financing the business; on the average it is no more than 2s. 6d. a head, or, in the aggregate, 0·8 per cent. of the total liabilities, and 0·4 per cent. of turnover.

In the older societies, the qualifying share capital for membership is usually only 1s. to 2s.; in the more recent this has been increased to 10s. The 1927 amendment of the Act has certainly paved the way for raising these amounts, but a serious psychological obstacle is still encountered in the conviction that has grown up amongst the members that shares ought to be, need to be, small. Already the 1926 Congress has rejected the Supervisory Council's proposal to increase the share to £1 minimum, to rise in time to £2 10s.

1930 Congress recommended societies to discontinue credit for their capital's sake, to cover at least the value of buildings, plant, etc., with their owned capital and their long-term loans, to be prudent in the purchase of property, to limit stocks to a maximum of 20 per cent. of the turnover, to prefer long-term loans, to allocate not less than half of any surplus to the funds, and to raise the share qualification to at least £1 10s.

While most of the net surplus is assigned to reserves, dividend ranging usually between 1 and 2 per cent. on purchases, and about 60 per cent. of the societies paying none at all, the K.K. like the S.O.K. societies religiously keep down prices and therefore surplus, and so much time must elapse before reserves can completely finance the trade. In 1928 the total assets were £4,000,000, of which share capital plus reserves totalled £1,070,000, or 26·8 per cent. of liabilities. In 1922 the proportion was only 18·9 per cent.

The other capital required is obtained from two main sources—loans from banks and credit from merchants on the one hand, and the savings and advances of members on the other. The former amounted in 1920 to 73·5 per cent. of the liabilities, but has been steadily reduced to 34·4 per cent. in 1929, or £1,375,000, of which £900,000 is credit from suppliers. To facilitate this reduction, saving has been strongly encouraged among the members, more especially as the accumulated resources of families also melted in the inflation, making the resuscitation of individual saving more than ever necessary.

Most K.K. societies have now their own Savings Departments, entitled to receive deposits, but not from non-members. The balance of these deposits has increased from £107,000 in 1920 to £1,550,000, and their proportion in the capital of societies from 6·8 to 38·8 per cent. As in the case of S.O.K. societies, the State forgoes its control of these Savings Departments in favour of OTK—the Wholesale Society—which supervises and verifies postings in detail and members' transactions, stimulates the interest of depositors, and nurses the sound development of the Savings movement. Neither wholesale has, however, any Savings Department of its own.

Inflation brought one advantage: the older mortgages could be repaid, and new buildings and sites acquired while their real price was lower than at present. This has considerably assisted co-operative development. Instead of heavy and speculative outlay in modernising rented premises, purchase or building has been preferred. In general, both the older properties and those recently acquired have been included in K.K. balance-sheets at present current values. Land and buildings and fixed and rolling stock accounted for £1,915,000, or 47·9 per cent. of total resources in 1928, stocks for £1,600,000 or 40·1 per cent. Mortgages amounted to £262,000 only.

In proportion as capital becomes easier and societies can safely depend on their own, they can expand and rationalise to a greater extent. Much has already been done. In Helsingfors, which, with its suburbs, has a population of 220,000, Elanto has in twenty-four years enrolled 41,000 members, representing 164,000 individuals or thereabouts; in Uleåborg, with 23,000 population, the K.K. society counts 11,000 members, and caters therefore for some 44,000; besides this an S.O.K. society also exists in the town, of 2,100 members, representing 8,400 mouths.

This apparently strange excess of co-operators over inhabitants in the proportion of two to one is explained by the fact that the K.K. society in Uleåborg works in 15 parishes. The figures are, however, signal proof of the appeal that co-operative societies and co-operation and their advantages make to the population in these areas as in so many other parts of Finland. In these regions private trade occupies a comparatively insignificant position. There are whole parishes in which such trade is non-existent.

K.K. societies, like S.O.K., have consistently opposed consumer credit, and sell as a rule for cash. The total of individuals' indebtedness to societies at the close of 1929 was under £21,000, or 0·3 per cent. of turnover; group debts aggregated 0·4 per cent. Vicious habits are not yet quite eradicated, though the conviction fast gains ground that cash trading is essential for sound household economy. Times have changed since Helsingfors workers founded their first co-operative in 1883, and definitely recognised credit (up to a certain sum) in their rules, believing this to be to the members' advantage and one of the objects for which a society ought to be formed.

The "Progressive" Central Union

The Progressive section started with a twofold organisation, a trading wholesale, OTK, on the one hand, and an educational and propaganda central union, K.K., on the other. The latter, dating from 1917, conducts educational work among members and staffs, and propaganda, advises in business management and law, audits and even trades in office equipment, besides shaping the movement's policy and watching over consumer interests generally. For these purposes K.K. is sectioned into departments for propaganda, study, publicity, education, employment agency, building (with full-time architects), legal advice, sales, and library and records.

The propaganda department employs a staff of seven, who cover the country the whole year round. Others of K.K. officials lend an occasional hand or voice. In 1929, 985 lectures were delivered by K.K. emissaries to audiences of 276,000 in all; 406 other public lectures and addresses were given on local initiative to 68,000 listeners. Impressive figures! Programmes are opulent, and varied to attract as many as possible, and the film is enlisted to an ever-increasing extent.

Special films have been shot to display the movement's activities and establishments, and to emphasise their importance and to stimulate saving. The distribution of literature in the form of leaflets, pamphlets, and books, mainly published by K.K. itself, accompanies most lectures. An annual special propaganda week has recently been arranged with lectures, exhibitions, social gatherings, and other attractions.

Lately K.K. have begun organising housewives for co-operative propaganda in the form of Women's Committees, working in conjunction with manager or secretary of the society. There were in 1929 about forty such committees engaged mainly in spreading knowledge in the household of the value of consumer co-operation, confuting slander and misrepresentation spread by unscrupulous competitors, teaching the children the significance of co-operation and encouraging thrift.

The Importance of Staff Training

Staff training becomes daily more essential and more exacting as the field of co-operation widens, and as charge of the growing number of branch shops, some at considerable distance from headquarters, calls for resource, decision, and initiative. A stream of capable recruits to the management corps is necessary in the interests of the movement and its progress.

Professional training, based on correspondence tuition, is undertaken by the educational department. Three such courses, with certain subjects compulsory on all, are in continuous process: elementary or apprentice, branch managers', and executive and control committees'. In the autumn of 1929 a course was begun in trade in agricultural produce and requirements.

At the end of 1929 there were 2,187 students taking correspondence courses:

11,66 in Stage I
337 in Stage II
272 in Stage III
412 in Stage IV

Staff training is further promoted by a series of oral classes which K.K. arranges every year. First there were autumn classes for future managers, branch and general, and longer classes, 3½ months, for bookkeepers. Later a few shorter courses were added for certain groups. Since 1930 these longer courses have been discontinued, and short periods of instruction in various trades are given during 4 or 5 months. Some are held every year, some every other year, others at longer intervals.

In 1930, for example, there were

a 3 days' lecture course for managers
a 10 days' course for junior managers
a 5 weeks' course for branch managers
a 4 weeks' course for butchery managers and assistants
a 2 weeks' course for storekeepers
a 2 weeks' course for grocery assistants

Besides these, all held in Helsingfors, about twenty-five lecture courses in the year are conducted in the provinces for staffs and management committees. The leader is usually a headquarters official, and the subjects relate to business affairs and educational activity.

Complementary to these is arranged every summer a fortnight's tour for employees, limited to twenty-five in number. Scenic charm is combined with progressive co-operative centres, whose managers explain their aims and methods, and where experiences are usefully exchanged. The tour of 1929 began at Sordavala in East Finland, continued to Volama Monastery on Lake Ladoga, on to the famous Punkaharju Ridge, then to Nyslott, by boat to Payana in North Finland, thence by motor along the Ule river to Uleåborg, and via Tammerfors to Helsingfors.

AUDIT; PROPERTY

Audit of societies' accounts falls also to K.K. education department, as does advice concerning business and management, on new branches, new departments of trade, etc. Every society sends in monthly trade statements, and every society has, further, voluntarily affiliated to K.K. specially for audit. Five trained accountants are employed. The audit is centralised, which allows the auditors to specialise along selected lines. Thus one is a stocks expert. If a monthly statement shows excessive stocks, this auditor can be despatched to the society at fault, to investigate and to suggest remedy. At present K.K.'s educational department sends to those co-operatives in its membership whose results are unsatisfactory—in number about fifty at time of writing—suggested costings for their shops and productive establishments. Thanks to so efficient and complete a system, K.K. societies survived without a single disaster all the crash and calamity of post-war times.

The Works Department is another immensely useful auxiliary. Advice is readily tendered whenever societies think of buying or building property, and designs and plans are prepared and submitted. In this department there are three architects, one draughtsman, and one consumer co-operative general manager to see that designs do not become fantastic, but serve efficiently their business and trading purposes.

Mention must be made also of K.K.'s legal department. This attends to societies' taxation difficulties and other troubles with the law. K.K. employs one lawyer exclusively for contracts and agreements on societies' behalf, who assists in preparing and considering such agreements and in negotiations with trade unions, etc., and expounds collective agreements for and to the executive.

Worthy of special note is the fact that K.K. Congress has decided that societies purchasing or building property, starting branches or productive enterprises, or extending business in any other way, negotiating collective agreements, or engaging a new manager, ought to inform and consult K.K. executive. Almost without exception this is done and the advice given followed.

A Great and Powerful Press

K.K. also issues the Progressive wing's newspapers, a splendid form and type of propaganda and education, at the same time waging the fight in protection of consumers' interests.

Two popular newspapers are published: *Kuluttajain Lehti* (*Consumers' Press*) in Finnish, weekly, with 130,000 circulation, and a Swedish counterpart, *Konsumentbladet* (meaning the same), twice a month for the ten or so societies in South-West Finland, Vasa, and Jakobstad, with a large proportion of Swedish-speaking members. As the circulation figures suggest, the contents are a judicious and appetising blend of information—co-operative and other—instruction and entertainment. Columns are reserved for housewives' interests, for children, and for the illustrated exploits of a very popular knockabout comedian—a Finnish Silly Billy—Pekka Puupää in his own tongue (Peter Woodenhead). Other Swedish-speaking co-operators take the Swedish edition of *Elanto*, the newspaper published by the celebrated Helsingfors society of that name.

For some years now K.K. has issued two special papers: *Työtoveri* (*Workmates*), in 6,000 copies, a technical organ for staffs, and *Osuusliike* (*The Co-operative Society*), in 3,200 copies, for supervisory councils and executives. And K.K. further sells office equipment and its own manufactures: boxes, sale checks, etc., to an amount of £95,000 in the year.

Management of K.K.; District Executives

K.K.'s government consists of the Annual Congress, Supervisory Council and Executive. The first directs policy and outlines development, reviews the year's results, and decides future action. Each society may send one representative to Congress, with, however, voting power proportional to the membership of his society. Thus one vote is allowed for every 200 or part thereof, so long as the membership does not exceed 5,000. After that, and up to 10,000, an additional vote is allowed for every 500 or part thereof. Beyond 10,000 a further additional vote is accorded for every 1,000 or part thereof. Thus the representative of Elanto with 41,000 members will have $(5{,}000 \div 200) + (5{,}000 \div 500) + (31{,}000 \div 1{,}000) = 25 + 10 + 31 =$ 66 votes.

Congress formally elects a Supervisory Council, whose members have, however, actually been nominated by the District Associations. The Supervisory Council then appoints an Executive, of whose six members and two substitutes only two are full-time officials. On the other hand, we may mention here that all the members of S.O.K. Executive are full-time officials.

There is a decentralised district organisation attending to local interests, development and propaganda, consisting of nine districts each, with its own executive elected annually in general meeting by representatives of the societies in each district.

OTK: Activities, Sales Organisation, Finance

The separation of function with which the Progressive movement began has allowed its Wholesale Society, OTK, to concentrate on trading activities, which is freely argued to have been of great advantage to its development.

Sales in 1918 were about £360,000; by 1920 they had reached almost £940,000, mounting to £3,575,000 in 1927, to £4,200,000 in 1928, and to £4,000,000 in 1929. OTK has five departments—grocery, manufactured goods, fancy goods, ironmongery, and agricultural commodities—the last-named supplying societies with, and selling direct, feeding stuffs, manures, machinery, etc., and buying in farm produce from societies—butter, eggs, oats, straw—to be resold to town societies. Distribution is effected through eight depots, with commodious and artistic show-rooms, in Helsingfors, Jyväskylä, Kuopio, Uleåborg, Tammerfors, Åbo, Vasa, Viborg, with a warehouse in Björneborg. Several of these are housed in OTK's own premises, among which most notable is the magnificent eleven-storey central warehouse in Helsingfors, with a floor area of 13,150 square yards, erected by K.K.'s own works department.

Societies are extremely loyal to OTK, some buying up to 80 and 90 per cent. of their requirements therefrom. Of the 111 societies no fewer than 26 bought over 75 per cent. of their whole turnover, 78 from 50 to 75 per cent., and 7 from 25 to 50 per cent. Remembering the production societies themselves carry on, these are admirable figures. Most of them advise K.K. and OTK monthly of all their purchases from other sources, with the names of suppliers. OTK examines these statements and comments thereon when necessary. The wholesale is thus kept in close touch with price movements, enabling it to make its competition keen and effective.

No higher surplus is budgeted than 3 to 3½ per cent., and of this three-fourths goes to reserve. Generally, indeed, the balance goes the same way. Share capital is trifling in amount, and borrowed money is therefore necessary. So the ambition is quite laudable to continue funding until independence of other capital, especially of banks and merchant credits, is attained.

With surplus then allocated, reserves in 1928 amounted to £370,000 and share capital £12,000, against total assets of £1,130,000. Almost two-thirds of the liabilities, £700,000, consist of loans on bond, bank loans, debt to merchants, acceptances, and other outside credits. The assets, however, include buildings, sites, and other resources acquired under favourable conditions, sound stocks, and valuable fixed and rolling stock, so that OTK is very healthy financially.

OTK Production and its Future

Lack of capital has, of course, restrained production. The rapid and disturbing progress of the Swedish Match Trust on Finland's match market, by means of purchase of all available Finnish match factories, sometimes in one name, sometimes in another, decided OTK in 1923 to erect its own factory. Machinery was procured, but manufacture could not be commenced till 1925. The site is at the foot of the delightful Pyynikki Hills, near Tammerfors, with abundance of poplar wood close by, and the output achieved is 46,000 cases in the year. Probably either of the two co-operative factories could alone meet the whole Finnish co-operative demand, and the conditions wrung from the Trust on capitulation, which allow S.O.K. and OTK together to fix the home retail price, prove that the fight was not all in vain. Surplus production, however, according to the settlement with the Trust, can only be sold abroad through one of the Trust's sale agencies.

Besides the match factory, OTK owns a rye-mill in Jääski, in Karelen, milling up to 80 tons a day, a clothing and linen factory in Helsingfors making hosiery, tablecloths, serviettes, gents' suits, and overcoats, also a chemical sundries factory and a coffee-mill in Helsingfors, and four herring saltings on the shores of the Gulf of Bothnia.

In the early summer of 1930, OTK began to manufacture margarine in its new and modern-equipped factory, reaching 100 tons a month by the end of the year. The output capacity is twice that amount, and room remains for plant to increase up to 400.

In this connection may be mentioned that the Anglo-Dutch Uni-Lever Trust has stretched its tentacles even over Finland. With the exception of the S.O.K. and OTK factories, and one or two small works owned by retailers, all the margarine factories in the country are reported to be under the Trust's control. All bears witness to the speed at which the Trust is moving to secure complete domination.

A large flour-mill is planned in Viborg, the present mill at Jääski having long been inadequate to meet the demand.

The industrial headquarters of OTK will still remain in Helsingfors. On Tavastgatan (Tavast Street) a large site is still owned and available, close to Elanto's headquarters and factories. Here are to be erected, according to programme, in the next few years a common headquarters for OTK and K.K., and the Progressive Insurance Societies, besides the margarine factory, to companion the laboratory, coffee-mill, and spice-packing factory, the chemical sundries, and minor workshops already there.

Along with Elanto's adjoining property the site covers nearly 60,000 square yards in the heart of the city, so that the two organisations between them bid fair to rear a co-operative citadel in the very centre of Finland's capital. There already the spires of Elanto's offices pierce the heavens, while, more prosaic, the bakery, meat factory, mineral-water factory, creamery, and warehouse nestle round. OTK's big central warehouse is so far its largest building (eleven storeys), but daily the walls of the new margarine factory seem to threaten its supremacy, and ample space still remains.

The inner organisation of OTK is similar to that of K.K. Congress is held at the same time as K.K.'s annual general meeting, and, by means of inter-representation on Supervisory Councils and executives, contact between the two organisations is assured and maintained.

CHAPTER VI

A MODEL CO-OPERATIVE SOCIETY: "ELANTO", HELSINGFORS

The Finnish dictionary relates the word "Elanto" to another Finnish word, "elämä", meaning "life", and "elanto" betokens all that is required for the decent maintenance of existence. This significance of the word has been deeply impressed on the minds of Helsingfors people during the quarter-century of Elanto's career. Scarcely one household necessity can be named that is not to be got in Elanto, and in its own factories the Society manufactures very many of these commodities itself, with no external help. It has enmeshed the city and its environs in a network of shops. A few yards from the Central Station the visitor meets a row of them, and thence outwards there is no quarter, suburb, or near-by village where the characteristic emblem of the society, the bee and the marguerite, is not prominent in the picture.

Elanto sells grocery, meat, milk, bread, boots, clothing, hosiery, dresses, millinery, cloth, household utensils, all in special shops, and in its Grand Magasin, a big central store in one of the finest and busiest streets: Broholmsgatan.

Quite often an Elanto shop is sighted with a red cross on the window. That is one of Elanto's drug shops, in which medicines, drugs, perfumes, soap, and other similar articles may be had.

But Elanto goes farther and carries on an extensive restaurant trade. All classes meet in its cafés, easily the best in Helsingfors, of popular type, comfortable, speckless, cheap. "Go to Elanto!" is a daily injunction in thousands of Helsingfors households whenever anything is short in kitchen or larder; and "Let us go to Elanto!" is the glad and welcome suggestion when friends are met to spend a happy hour together.

Elanto's motors and vehicles are from morn till night the most familiar feature of the city streets, and the average Helsingfors citizen mentally ranks the Society as an indispensable adjunct of town-life, like gas, water, or electricity; and yet Elanto is but in its youth.

A Neutral Society, Open to All

The Society was started October 15, 1905, at a meeting in the Students' Hostel in Helsingfors. Nineteen members were enrolled and £7 7s. of share capital subscribed. Membership was left open to all. Earlier attempts in the city had been confined to certain classes such as railwaymen, or to certain groups working in the same mill or factory. The name usually indicated as much, and sometimes the rules, as in the earliest attempt by Palmén in 1866, deliberately excluded workers. In turn, Helsingfors Workers' Co-operative, founded 1903, adopted a constitution which no non-Socialist could accept.

Any tendency in this direction has been rigorously avoided by Elanto, which explains, no doubt, much of its success. The aforementioned Workers' Co-operative and others of similar character have all been converted to Elantoism, and have been glad to join Elanto. There are now only two other consumer co-operatives in the capital: Varuboden and Helsingin Osuuskauppa, the former exclusively for Swedish-speaking members, and both belonging to the S.O.K. group.

Elanto's size, especially in regard to available population, justly entitles it to recognition as the premier society in the north. Stockholm Society has more members, more sales, but drawn from a population twice as great. Elanto has now 42,000 members, 8,000 of them Swedish-speaking, and an annual turnover of £1,700,000. Including the 9,500 members of the other two societies there are thus some 51,000 families co-operatively organised in Helsingfors, or, allowing for double membership, at least 70 per cent. of its whole population.

The operations of the Society are not confined to the city; its shops are to be seen in nine communes outside the boundaries. By far the greater part of the membership are yet townsfolk. About 60 per cent. are industrial workers, 20 per cent. business employees, 10 per cent. officials and business proprietors, and 5 per cent. from the professional classes.

Shops: Central Premises, Building Plans, Restaurants

Elanto owns quite a number of manufacturing enterprises, and the buildings they occupy, both in town and country. The total number of shops in 1930 was 235, of cafés and restaurants 12, and the number of employees was 2,350. These with their families could people a whole town, which would not be Finland's smallest.

Reference has been made already to the high standard of Elanto shops, and their influence on co-operative shop art and science in Finland can scarcely be exaggerated. Fine taste and ingenious adaptation, fruit of long experience, are outstanding features. Indeed, the latest, in the new middle-class suburb Tölö, and in the new property in Tavastgatan, are probably not excelled by any co-operative society anywhere. Meat shops are provided with chill-rooms and cupboards, floors and ceilings consist of light-tinted, easily washed glazed tiles or marble, and special attention is given to sufficient and effective ventilation in cellars and warehouses. Nor are milk and grocery shops one whit behind.

The well-trained and educated staffs in all the shops speak fluently both the country's languages. In the drug shops there are specially qualified compounders, many with pharmaceutical certificates.

A new magasin or departmental store is planned for the corner of Glo and Alexander Streets, a central position. Elanto secured this site some years ago, and already has shops in the properties acquired with and on the site. Many of the Society's shops in Helsingfors, and most of those outside, occupy premises owned by Elanto. Where this has proved impossible, accommodation has been sought, and generally obtained, in Building Society properties.

The trading area extends 18 miles east to west and 19 north to south. The smaller societies serving this area have mostly been absorbed by Elanto, which has remodelled or reconstructed their premises and opened new branches. The present spacious and handsome shops, with the bee and marguerite bedecking their signboards, contrast violently with the mean, dilapidated premises of the remaining private traders.

The first of Elanto's restaurants was opened in August 1908, to the same superior grins that met the Rochdale weavers when they took down their shutters. Strong drink was banned, contrary to the general practice then in Helsingfors cafés; and in a few months the place could not accommodate its trade.

The customers included workers and students, writers and artists, and soon the rooms became a favourite resort of the educated and intellectual. The Elanto restaurants of to-day resemble very little that first modest venture in the low wooden house in Michel Street, but the clientèle remains much the same: scholars, workers, students, clerks, employees. With their light and airy, flower-decorated halls and rooms, equipped generally with loud-speakers, their popularity shows no wane. In the banking and commercial quarters they are the best-patronised lunch-rooms. In others, of our "eating-house" type, the worker in his dungarees can take his hurried meal, feeling quite at home.

The Society Which Will Manufacture All Itself

Elanto's own productions have long exceeded the half of its sales. Its first manufacturing venture was a bakery, and subsequent additions to the list have clustered round the bakery as the parent cell of the hive.

The first bakery, erected 1907, was commodious, hygienic, and up to date for that time, but its capacity did not long suffice, and extension became necessary. The next bakery, the present, was ready in March 1925. This is 195 ft. long by 90 ft. wide and 100 ft. high, with six storeys and four intermediate floors, with 21 large ovens, mostly with several drawplates, 100 electrical machines: automatic dough dividers, moulders, kneaders, mixers, etc., cold storage, own transformer station, etc.

Soft bread, hard bread, Vienna bread, and pastry are baked by processes almost completely mechanised. Machinery conveys the grain up to the mill, mills it, carries the flour to the bins, weighs it, and passes it on to the doughing machine, kneads the dough, and rolls it along to the mechanical divider, which cuts it up into the desired weight and forms the pieces into loaves. The hard-bread ovens are of the travelling type, where the chunks of dough enter on an endless moving plate, and come out baked and finished.

Finally, the baked bread is despatched to the shops in motors summoned from the caverns of a subterranean garage, where they have been spending the night. The bakery has its own laboratory, where flour is examined, baking tests made, etc.

Before the new bakery came into operation even, Elanto was providing Helsingfors with one-third of its daily bread. The output capacity of the new bakery is about three times that of the old, and now 60 per cent. of the bread needs of the city are supplied therefrom.

On the factory site in Tavast Street, Elanto has also its creamery and its meat factory. The dairy, though new in 1911, has just been rebuilt, and now contains pasteurising plant, milk-cleaning and cooling apparatus and bottling machinery, butter-packing plant, cheese storage, etc. Little churning is done. Supplies of milk are drawn directly from the farmers and from co-operative creameries and milk-sale societies; butter and cheese from the co-operative creamery wholesale, Valio, with whom an understanding obtains which leaves the retail sale of milk in Helsingfors to the consumer co-operative.

Elanto thus provides an excellent example of direct relations between co-operative producers and co-operative consumers. The old bakery is now the meat factory, employing also all the latest machinery and still meeting the full demand of the membership. Elanto bottles all its own mineral waters and soft drinks in a factory adjoining.

The society engages in much other manufacture for its own service: equipment and upkeep shops and factories, such as engineering, joiners', painters', papering workshops, laundries, sewing-rooms, etc. Nor must its two farms be forgotten, one of which, Backas, is close to Helsingfors. Here are fed some of the many swine that later, in pork, ham, and sausage form, appear on Helsingfors breakfast-tables, a transformation attended with "many a grunt and shriek", to quote Karlfeldt, Sweden's poet-laureate.

"Bread and Circuses"; Contact with Members

Very different are the sounds from the Society's other land holding—the island of Sumparn, just outside the harbour—rented from the city. This is the summer resort of the staff and their children, the latter being run out every morning by motor-boat and handed over to a jolly "aunt". Elanto may well claim to be a model employer also, assisting its workers to acquire homes of their own, and studying their interests and welfare in many other respects.

In the new central premises sick-nurses are installed for the benefit of the factory staffs, and in a well-equipped clinic a doctor is in attendance every day. Gymnastics and sports are encouraged, and in return the athletes and dancers give displays to the members in their fine new hall. Elanto's girl gymnasts and dancers, all shop assistants or factory hands, are well known and appreciated by Elanto membership.

Amateur theatricals also find vogue, and a first performance was recently given in the same hall, when Strindberg's *The Father* was played. The employees have, besides, a brass band, social clubs, and many other similar institutions.

For some years now Elanto's government has been on a representative basis. The Supervisory Council, elected by the delegates chosen by the members by areas, contains representatives of all classes: workers, officials, journalists, housewives, professors, and other occupations and professions; Socialist, Conservative, Communist, Swedish-speaking, Finnish-speaking. Oskari Mantere, ex Prime Minister of Finland, is Vice-President of the Supervisory Council, and at one and the same time, some years ago, several Cabinet Ministers sat round its table.

Beside the Supervisory Council and the Managing Executive, function Shop Committees, which have regular general meetings, and are of high importance in maintaining contact with the members. Elanto's newspaper, with a circulation of 29,000 in Finnish and Swedish editions, is of much assistance in the same direction. This was started in 1916, and has given excellent service both to education and propaganda, and both in Elanto and elsewhere.

Regular series of educational and propaganda meetings are arranged with lectures, songs, instrumental music, plays and sketches, and other entertainment, usually in Elanto's own hall, which is provided with suitable scenery. So does Elanto help different classes to know and understand each other, and help to close the gaps and smooth the differences between those of different political creeds.

The name "Elanto" is inseparably bound up with that of one of Finland's best-known men in international co-operative circles, Väinö Tanner, also a former Prime Minister. For fifteen years he has been Managing Director, and to his prudent, clear-sighted, firm control is very largely to be ascribed the fact that all through the storms which shook the movement in the great crisis of the Civil War of 1918 the Society remained intact and united.

Only when Väinö Tanner was Prime Minister has the management been out of his hands. Tirelessly he has toiled to make Elanto, to extend it, to enthuse the members in its cause and for the movement, to teach them, to build up a model co-operative which should draw the whole movement onward and upward in its wake. In this way, and by virtue of his vast and beneficent influence on the "progressive" movement, Väinö Tanner has become the foremost representative of modern co-operation in Finland, and, in consequence, Elanto has not been merely a successful big society, but something greater, nobler. No story of Finland's co-operation can, therefore, be nearly complete without one chapter at least on Elanto.

CHAPTER VII

THE CO-OPERATIVE SUPPLY OF AGRICULTURAL REQUISITES THROUGH "HANKKIJA" AND "LABOR"

The needs of a farmer's household are now many and various; the old days are gone of the self-provided steading. Specialisation has invaded even agriculture, and the modern farmer has to study what branches of production he can in his case make pay best and concentrate on them.

The Danish peasant, as all know, devotes his attention to milk and butter for the market, nourishing himself the while on margarine. So in Sweden in many districts bread-grain growing has ceased to be profitable, and farmers have turned to fodder-grain crops for the market, feeding and dairying and buying flour with the proceeds.

We have seen how Finnish farmers in exemplary manner have organised the supply of their consumption goods through their consumer co-operatives, which in turn organised to procure supplies from their wholesales. Consumer co-operatives sell agricultural requirements too, and the more specialised farming becomes the greater grows the need for such requisites and appliances: machinery, manures, and feeding stuffs especially. That societies handling these should purchase their supplies of farming requisites from private firms would be most illogical.

So alongside the consumer co-operative wholesales there has been found room for special Wholesale Societies for agricultural supplies, which also should undertake large-scale sale of farm produce, particularly grain—a natural development of their primary function. In Finland there are two such wholesales: Hankkija and Labor, fully equal in age with the consumer co-operative wholesales. Labor was actually founded originally in 1897.

FROM PELLERVO'S AGENCY TO HANKKIJA

The early and strenuous efforts of Pellervo, before consumer co-operation had taken root in the countryside, to arouse the interest of farmers and their guilds, then flourishing as agricultural supply associations, in the common purchase of requirements, have already been told. These guilds were, however, painfully dependent on private middlemen, and many were convinced that a wholesale for such common purchase was absolutely necessary if the whole co-operative idea was not to come to naught.

Pellervo started its agency for supplying farmers' guilds, co-operative creameries, Credit Banks, and other collective buyers in rural areas with agricultural requisites in 1901, buying from the larger private wholesales. While this undoubtedly denoted progress, results did not fulfil expectations, since the agency, suffering from want of capital, could not itself import or buy direct from the manufacturer.

In 1905, therefore, it was converted into a co-operative wholesale, Keskusosuusliike Hankkija, with 18 co-operative creameries, 27 Credit Banks, and 2 other co-operatives as original members. The subscribed capital amounted to £190 only, and beginning had to be made on a very modest scale and very cautiously. The office staff consisted of manager and two assistants, while an errand boy was shared with S.O.K. Trusting to the superiority of the co-operative form of trading, a bold yet prudent start was made, and the trust was not betrayed. To-day Hankkija is the leading business of its kind in the country, and, with Labor, dominates completely the sale of certain agricultural commodities.

A large and very important trade has also been developed as contractor for rural electrification, for the erection of co-operative creameries, saw-mills, moss-litter works, flour-mills, water supplies, etc. Hankkija, further, very effectively serves agriculture in general experimental work, grain culture and improvement, and seed cleaning, in all of which splendid results have been attained. Again, Hankkija subscribes to and aids a number of agricultural organisations, such as various farmers' central associations, cattle improvement societies, creamery unions, etc., contributing thereto on an average in recent years as much as £6,000 a year.

According to the original rules, Hankkija was to be a wholesale exclusively for co-operative associations, and no other membership was to be recognised. In 1908 individual membership was introduced, and farmers' guilds, until then not eligible, were allowed to join. In this way a closer connection of the guilds with Hankkija was encouraged and expected.

But from 1912 farmer guilds were not further accepted in membership; their credit was found quite unsatisfactory and their importance as suppliers had gone. The trade in agricultural requisites had passed into the hands of the country consumer co-operatives. Since 1921 individual membership has not been permitted, as it was considered that with the rise of these co-operatives farmers should purchase there. The rules have thus been modified to march with the progress of events, and Hankkija has now become once more strictly a wholesale for co-operative associations, as originally intended.

Hankkija's Membership, Trade, Finance

Consumer co-operatives, co-operative creameries and milk-sale societies, and co-operative Credit Banks form to-day the bulk of the membership. Seventy-five to 80 per cent. of the sales are made to consumer co-operatives, and the Credit Banks in particular may be regarded as merely supporting members. Co-operative creamery purchases are limited mainly to machinery, steam and electricity erections, appliances and plant; with the creamery wholesale, Valio, there exists a long-standing agreement that the designing and equipment of co-operative creameries shall be undertaken by both jointly.

Of the net trading surplus, 60 per cent. goes to reserves until these reach £130,000, already exceeded. In new rules, as yet in draft only, this limit is proposed to be raised to £520,000; 10 per cent. goes next to a Contingency Fund.

To be of the maximum immediate advantage to members, Hankkija cuts prices as fine as possible, troubling little about dividend. Should, however, there be at any time profits to distribute, members will share, on co-operative principle, in proportion to purchases made. Nor are there any rebates, so common in other countries.

The management of the business is all in the hands of an executive of five, appointed by the Supervisory Council of fifteen, who in turn are elected by the Annual General Meeting, at which every member has one vote.

Hankkija operates over the whole of Finland, with sale offices in Helsingfors, at its headquarters, and in Viborg, Åbo, Vasa, Tammerfors, Uleåborg, Björneborg, Kuopio, and Jyväskylä, and, without stocks, in five other centres. Some of these occupy buildings belonging to the Society itself. Total sales in 1928 were £1,950,000. The principal features of Hankkija's progress appear in the table on page 93.

As the figures show, reserves have accumulated very rapidly of late. Assets in 1928 amount to over £470,000, covered to the extent of nearly one-third by share capital and reserves. As in the case of the other whole-

TRADE AND PROGRESS OF HANKKIJA

Year.	Sales, in £1,000.	Membership.		Total.	Reserves, in £1,000.
		Number of Societies.	Others.		
1905	27	67	—	67	0·24
1910	144	236	122	358	14
1915	364	694	317	1,011	35
1920	1,300	1,014	290	1,304	101
1925	1,130	1,006	261	1,267	66
1926	1,440	1,003	254	1,257	83
1927	1,600	1,002	246	1,248	110
1928	1,950	996	241	1,237	148

sales, Hankkija's property and fixed stock are worth much more than the balance-sheet indicates, whose figures therefor have been carried forward from the days of dearer prices. So the financial position is much more favourable even than the statement shows. The whole of the productive establishments are entered at £7,200, the business premises at £52,000, and the experimental estate, Tammisto, at £5,000.

A tight rein has always been kept on credit sales. Hankkija, like the other wholesales, refers its customers to the agricultural credit institutions for accommodation. True, outstanding debts of members appear as £109,000 in the latest report, or something like 6 per cent. of the turnover, but these largely refer to big building contracts in process for co-operative creameries, electricity societies, and other associations. The amount owing for goods was insignificant. Hankkija sells generally on three months' terms, but allows so generous discount that the members find cash payment much more advantageous. Within the next few years the management hope to eliminate credit altogether; much depends in this respect on the progress of co-operative Credit Banking.

Sales Organisation and Direct Productions

Hankkija operates in five departments: manures and feeding stuffs, grain, seeds, machinery, and electrical, each purchasing, importing, exporting, and distributing to depots its own goods and services. There are also educational and accounting departments.

The name sufficiently indicates the scope of each department. For the first, oil-cake is ground in the Society's own mill at Malm, outside Helsingfors. The grain department buys from member societies and finds a market, milling some in its Tammerfors mill —2,000 tons in 1928—and selling part to private or other co-operative mills. The turnover of this department depends upon the crop; the failure of 1928 reduced sales on the previous year by 34 per cent. Several member societies have, as already noted, grain silos of their own with treating and storing facilities, and this meets with Hankkija's firm approval, since prices naturally depend upon good and even quality.

In judging the value of Hankkija as a grain-sales agency, the general insignificance of the wholesale trade in home-grown grain in Finland must be borne in mind; this rarely exceeds 35,000 to 40,000 tons in the year, of which rye accounts for some 12,000 and oats 20,000 tons; the rest is made up of wheat and barley.

The largest purchaser of native grain is the State Granary, established in 1928 to provide for the Army and all other State institutions, and buying from consumer co-operatives, other dealers, and from the larger growers. S.O.K. also purchases direct from consumer co-operatives for its flour-mills. Hankkija's function has thus become the direction of supplies from the co-operative societies collecting, to the mills, co-operative and other, in the consuming areas. While, therefore, largely middleman, it undertakes credit risk, especially important for the small buyer. And, at its own cost, Hankkija publishes statements of grain on offer.

Hay and straw are handled similarly, at exceedingly moderate charges.

The chief object of this activity is to promote the sale of home-grown produce. Quality standards conform in part to those imposed by the State Granary. Most of the grain received by co-operatives is in very small parcels: 50 to 60 stone, and is paid for direct; only larger consignments are bought on the wholesale's account.

Tammisto: A Milestone in the Development of Finnish Agriculture

Hankkija not only sells grain for its members, but labours to increase the productivity of grain cultivation. Experiments in this direction were begun in 1913 on the estate of an interested practical agriculturist, but in 1916 a farm was purchased for the purpose in Helsinge parish, outside Helsingfors. This property, Tammisto (the Oak Wood), of 150 acres arable, neighbours Elanto's farm Backas. To the original buildings have been added a three-storey laboratory, a kiln, a threshing-floor, various farm buildings, and a silo series with the latest drying apparatus.

The selection of seed varieties here worked out suitable to Finland's soil and climate has been singularly profitable. In charge is Dr. J. O. Sauli, Finland's leading expert in seed culture. All the more important grains, and many garden vegetables, are under constant study and trial. Samples are gathered in from all quarters of the country, tried out in test-plots, and the best of these local growths are subsequently crossed with approved foreign varieties of known high yield and cold resistance. Reports and experiences are exchanged with similar institutions abroad.

New strains have been successfully introduced for both spring and autumn sowings, combining hardihood and yield in a manner that has increased the value of grain production by hundreds of thousands of pounds sterling a year. Special success has attended the endeavour to improve oats, but barley, wheat, rye, hay, and vegetables have all responded generously to attention.

At least four superior varieties of oats, three of barley, and two of wheat have been given to Finland, and have achieved great popularity. The new strains are first firmly established at Tammisto; then, to produce sufficient for trade, parcels are given out on cultivation contracts to experienced grain-growers. Agreement has been made with the State experimental department that no new seed shall be placed upon the market until there have been at least three years of comparison of crops from such seed grown either on the State experimental farm, or on those of some of the local testing stations in various parts of the country. In 1928 contract cultivation extended to nearly 3,000 acres.

The importance of this contribution to national wealth by Hankkija is difficult fully to realise, and the stranger signs the visitors' book in the laboratory at Tammisto with feelings of admiration and respect. There he finds names of noted experts from all corners of the earth, testimony to the interest with which the work of this institution is everywhere followed.

The long view is peculiarly necessary here; many patient years of unremitting care are required definitely to prove the value of new strains, and, however good the results, final satisfaction still eludes. "Nothing is so good, but it can be better", is Dr. Sauli's motto.

Until 1923 Hankkija carried on Tammisto unaided: since that year the State has contributed £1,550 a year, which of course still leaves much to pay.

Tammisto seed is sold all over Finland, and, early in its history, modern cleaning apparatus was necessary to treat the quantities demanded. A separate establishment, a fine five-storey building with every facility, was provided for this purpose in 1919 at Tammerfors. The seed is first carefully tested, after drying if necessary. A crushing-mill for discarded seed is part of the equipment.

The grain is cleaned and sorted according to weight, diameter, and length, and all transport is effected, as befits a modern institution of the kind, by mechanical hoists and travelling conveyers. Grass seeds are also treated, with special machinery. Near Tammerfors, Hankkija has also a flour-mill turning out rye flour and oatmeal.

For ten years Hankkija has had its own nursery gardens in Turenki, where fruit trees, berry bushes, decorative plants, and vegetables are grown and new strains evolved. These as well are sold by the seeds department, which, like the rest of the departments, has its own staff education and training section.

Much has been done to enlighten the farmer on the importance of seed of good and known pedigree. Leaflets have been published, lectures held, and salesmen have lost no opportunity of discussing the subject with the farmers they serve. This department has been especially active advocating and promoting revision of the law relating to trade in seeds and its control. All Hankkija's seed trade and activity is subject to control by the State's seed department.

Hankkija's Machinery Department the Largest in Finland

The machinery department both sells agricultural machinery and undertakes building construction, and is the largest establishment of its kind in Finland. At

Hankkija's twentieth-year celebrations in 1925 its record included planning, erection, and equipment of 300 creameries, 350 flour-mills, 200 saw-mills and timber yards, and a large number of smaller household sawing plants, with 50 other productive installations to meet the needs of farmers, such as mechanical driers. Many water supplies have also been installed.

In recent years a number of larger contracts of various kinds have been undertaken—for example, the refitting of Tuotanto bakery in Tammerfors. All the larger creameries have been built by Hankkija, including those belonging to Valio, Elanto, and the Farmers' Milk Central in Helsingfors. And all the machinery in S.O.K.'s big new mill at Uleåborg has been supplied by Hankkija.

The electrical department has installed most of the rural electrification in Finland. At the same celebrations this department was stated to have built 215 electricity works, large and small, including several power stations, and much cable work running to 3,750 miles of high-tension and low-tension lines and 750 transforming stations.

This department has had to fight rings formed to manipulate tenders, which makes its success the more remarkable and valuable to the whole public. Especially in agricultural machinery, dairy construction, etc., has Hankkija had salutary effect in restriction of prices and in restoration of genuine competition, and the reintroduction of fair play in tendering.

As a striking example of the efficiency of Hankkija may be cited the fact that, in conjunction with the co-operation creameries, it has so rationalised the supply of their requirements that, although, for instance, Danish co-operative dairies have similar joint arrangements, and although the necessary beech-wood is grown in Denmark but not in Finland, butter casks are actually cheaper in Finland than in Denmark.

And, in general, butter-packing costs are no more than half those in neighbouring countries.

For both agricultural machinery and many other articles Hankkija is the recognised agent in Finland of the largest, most reputable foreign firms. In this direction Hankkija has started production itself. A few years back the Society acquired all the shares in the Agricultural Machinery Company and its factory at Malm near Helsingfors. There threshing mills are manufactured, also chaff-cutters, sowing machines, steam boilers, and smaller dairy machinery, cheese-making apparatus, etc. Hankkija's threshing mills enjoy special reputation.

Education and Training in Hankkija

Hankkija's educational work is very similar to that of Y.O.L. and K.K., and includes instruction on the general importance of co-operation to agriculture, and in the trade in agricultural requirements and products, and publishing. The educational department collects and circulates statistics, arranges classes, and advises generally, though here the separate trading departments play the more prominent part.

The District Councils assist in the educational work as do the sale depot staffs and occasional teachers. Special attention is given to imparting knowledge of the trade in agricultural requirements to the assistants in country consumer co-operatives. In 1928 there were one- or two-day schools held in eleven districts and attended by 541 pupils. Threshing-mill classes, electricity classes, and others of special character have also been arranged along with the District Councils.

Since 1921 a one-month school has been run each year for co-operative branch managers, giving special training in agricultural trading. Summer schools and tours are planned to bring consumer co-operative staffs and executives into closer touch with Hankkija. Much lecturing is done; in 1928 some 200 addresses were delivered to audiences totalling 30,000. Hankkija has no newspaper of its own, but supports instead the Press of Pellervo, S.O.K., and other central co-operative organisations.

"Labor": Finland's Oldest Co-operative Central

The invaluable work done by Hankkija for the centralisation of co-operative trade in agricultural requirements finds remarkable complement in the Wholesale Society *Labor*, operating in the Swedish-speaking areas. Labor is older than Hankkija.

Over forty years ago farmers in Helsinge parish, near Helsingfors, discussed the formation of a co-operative society for the purchase of seed, manures, etc., and from their deliberations and subsequent committee work eventually sprang Labor. Rules were approved in 1897 entitling the effort to rank as the first co-operative association of farmers in Finland.

Individual membership is here the mainstay; no other kind was in sight in 1897. But local societies and guilds are quite eligible for admission. Labor was fortunate in retaining for many years its original managing director, J. Cygnaeus, M.A., whose energy and ability gave it prosperity and success. Since the Act relating to co-operative societies came into force, Labor has added "Co-operative Wholesale" to its title and has reorganised on co-operative lines.

From its inception, however, the society had transacted wholesale business, and in this respect, therefore, no change was necessary. At present there are on the roll 961 individual members, and 131 association members, and the turnover has steadily risen to £620,000. The first year's sales were £2,600; £40,000 was reached by 1902; by 1913 the figure was £180,000.

The rules enact that a certain proportion of the annual profit shall be allocated to reserve, and any dividend shall be distributed according to purchases made. At the end of 1928 reserves stood at £18,000, not excessive in relation to a value in total assets of £186,000. In this connection the effects of inflation have to be remembered. Of the 1928 surplus of £3,920, £3,875 went to reserves.

Labor a Special Wholesale for Swedish-speaking Districts

Labor was not originally intended to serve only the Swedish-speaking population. Its aim was rather to embrace the whole of Finland, irrespective of language or social distinctions. But among the founders and early leaders were many Swedish-speaking, and after the formation of Hankkija the Finnish-speaking tracts elected to concentrate their trade in the new society.

Labor, however, was rooted fast in the Swedish-speaking territory. Its members are very largely farmers, estate owners, and consumer co-operatives using that tongue in South and West Finland, round Helsingfors, and in Nyland, Åland, Åbo county, and Österbotten. So, naturally, Labor's sale depots and stores are in this region, at Helsingfors, Åbo, Vasa, Borgå, Lovisa, Mariehamn, Kristinestad, and Ekenäs, etc.

Production, Education, Publicity

Like Hankkija, Labor sells feeding stuffs, manures. seeds, and machinery, and has a building department. It owns two meal mills, one near Jorfvas, one at Borgå. Alongside the former, which is of quite recent date, Labor has also a flour-mill for milling the grain bought from members. Its feeding stuffs, whose manufacture is supervised by the well-known expert in cattle foods, Georg von Wendt, stand high in popular esteem. Labor has, besides, a seed control. Of the total turnover in 1928, £114,000 represented machinery, implements, and building work, £253,000 feeding stuffs, £109,000 manures, £44,000 seeds and grain, £48,000 building material, and £57,000 sundries.

Nor is education neglected. A newspaper in Swedish, *Labor*, is issued, excellent and appreciated alike for its general co-operative instruction and information, and for its technical agricultural contents. Labor co-operates with Finland's Swedish Central Union, whose secretary, R. Bremer, is also editor of *Labor*. Lectures on agricultural co-operative questions and on general agriculture are supplied by this department and educational classes arranged.

The system of government of Labor resembles Hankkija's. A Supervisory Council, elected by the Annual General Meeting, reviews the work of the Managing Executive, who attend to current business.

The Splendid Results of Agricultural Co-operation

Agricultural centralised sale and purchase, represented by Hankkija and Labor, have thus attained an extent and a success that far surpass the anticipations of the enterprising spirits who guided the first uncertain steps. The combined sales of the two in 1928 approached £2,600,000; they have given magnificent assistance to popular education, and rendered incalculable service to agricultural productivity. Hankkija alone transacts 40 per cent. of Finland's trade in manures, 30 per cent. of that in feeding stuffs, and 60 to 70 per cent. of that in seeds. The manner in which this last supremacy has been won is especially admirable. Of wholesale trade in agricultural machinery, Hankkija claims 45 per cent.; of that in creamery machinery no less than 90 per cent.

In this field the co-operative form of undertaking has proved itself clearly superior. Prices have been kept down, and ceaseless effort for the improvement of agriculture and agricultural methods has promoted the interests of the individual household far beyond what any figures available can illustrate. Great possibilities of development still exist in this sphere, especially in relation to the sale of agricultural produce. The big co-operative wholesale mills will surely become a valuable ally in pricing grain, notably bread grain.

In one direction, butter and cheese, the success achieved seems almost to touch conceivable limits. But, before we proceed to consider the creamery movement and its wonderful progress, won not least by its central wholesale organisation, Valio, some study will be appropriate of the co-operative activity that in many ways has staked and financed the boom in co-operative production, both in the co-operative creamery movement and elsewhere, i.e. Credit Co-operation, represented by the Co-operative Credit Banks, the marvellous creation of Professor Hannes Gebhard.

CHAPTER VIII

CO-OPERATIVE CREDIT BANKS

In 1862 the Mayor of the little German town of Weyerbusch, Friedrich Wilhelm Raiffeisen, founded the first Co-operative Credit Bank in the village of Anhausen, near Neu Wied, in Southern Germany. Its purpose was to provide credit on cheaper conditions to the poor distressed peasants in that region.

That tiny institution has been copied with phenomenal success all over the known world. In India there are fully 70,000 successors to-day. Admittedly the innovation has played a conspicuous part in agricultural progress towards greater productivity and in the economic salvation of the tiller of the soil.

Raiffeisen Basic Principles

Raiffeisen banks are based on personal credit—the confidence of the lender in the borrower. Help is to be found for those so poor or so straitened that they can lodge no real security. Small farms were so loaded with mortgages when Raiffeisen began his experiment that not another penny could be raised on them. He drew up a constitution for his new bank on the principle that "the poor ought to help each other, and to help themselves", or, in the paraphrase of Luigi Luzzati: "A bank is an institution where the money of the poor is lent out to the rich; a Co-operative Credit Bank an institution where the money of the poor is lent out to the poor."

Consequently Agricultural Credit Banks were to be built on a very moderate, even trifling, share qualification for membership, so that no one, however poor, would be hindered by his poverty from joining and participating in their services, and on joint and unlimited liability of the whole membership for their bank's obligations.

The circle of membership was to be so restricted for any one bank that all knew each other, their character and circumstances, not usually extending beyond one parish. Loans, according to Raiffeisen, were to be granted only for productive purposes, the bank to see that each loan was actually so applied. No division of profit among members and no remuneration of officials were to be considered. So expenses would be kept down, to the benefit of the bank and its clients.

Raiffeisen expected guides and leaders from the ranks of the priesthood, teachers, landed proprietors, Civil Service, and upper and educated classes generally, and believed that the consciousness of good works should to them be ample remuneration. Of the original Raiffeisen principles all are strictly observed in Finland, unless perhaps this last-mentioned. Not everywhere can outlay and expense be so rigorously avoided, but the general character and advantages of the Co-operative Credit movement are not impaired when the bank, for example, owns its own premises. The circumstances of to-day are so changed from those Raiffeisen knew that much then considered luxury is now time- and money-saving necessity.

Professor Gebhard introduces Raiffeisen Co-operation into Finland

When the movement reached Finland a quarter of a century ago, the same lamentable conditions prevailed there in agriculture as Raiffeisen had found in his own locality. Farms were heavily involved, and unscrupulous extortion was practised on the poor and miserable smallholders in East Finland to an extent that was arousing general concern.

During his stay in Germany in the nineties, Professor

Gebhard had made the acquaintance of the Raiffeisen movement, and perceived in it a remedy for this unhappy state of affairs. He was, however, convinced that to begin at the bottom and work upwards would be too slow, so he began with the establishment of a central organisation for systematic propaganda, and to provide material assistance to Credit Banks as and when they appeared.

So in 1902 the Central Credit Institution of Co-operative Credit Banks (Osuuskassojen Keskuslainarahasto-Osakeyhtiö or O.K.O.) was founded and immediately got busy. The first banks were started in Karelen and Savolaks, the districts whence came the most disturbing accounts of poverty and usury. In the next eight years on an average fifty to sixty banks a year came into existence. From 1911 to 1920 the rate abated; a considerable number had gone down through bad management, exciting the constant mistrust and suspicion of the Russian overlords. In 1918 the Civil War broke out and for a few years inflation raged rampant. None the less the movement continued to grow, if slowly; some twenty banks were added annually.

Special attention was attracted at this time to South-West Finland, where the cottars, claiming independence and ownership, began here and there to recognise the value of Co-operative Credit Banks. Following 1921 the movement received fresh impulse and 120 banks a year blossomed forth.

The increase was most marked in the cottar country: South-West Finland, Nyland, and Satakunta, particularly after the cottars had realised their ambition and carried the day. The Swedish-speaking areas, where, at first, proposals were very coldly received, began to grasp the value of co-operative credit. Then rapid development was seen in North Finland; the smallholders there, suffering under a succession of crop failures and bad harvests, were driven to this expedient, and now the Co-operative Credit Bank has penetrated right to Petsamo, away up on the Arctic coast, whither S.O.K. has now followed with a consumer co-operative.

In 1928 the State registration recorded, in all, 1,539 active Co-operative Credit Banks, of which 1,416 drew on the Central Credit Institution to an extent of £4,800,000 outstanding January 1, 1929. The general progress is well portrayed in the statistics:

Year.	Co-operative Credit Banks Drawing on O.K.O.	Number of Communes served.	Banks' Membership.
1903	10	7	284
1905	119	73	3,984
1910	374	144	17,496
1915	508	205	25,663
1920	602	248	31,080
1925	1,233	423	95,419
1926	1,344	457	108,763
1927	1,399	474	119,814
1928	1,416	477	130,145

The average membership is thus about eighty, quite according to Raiffeisen parish-pump standards.

Methods of Operation

Legally the Credit Banks (only Co-operative Credit Banks are included under this name here) are co-operative societies with unlimited liability, fulfilling thus another of the original essentials. On the other hand, one principle has so far been modified that share subscription of larger amount than suggested by Raiffeisen is required of the members: 6s. to 10s. The banks recently established prescribe the share qualification for membership as £1 10s. to £3 per member. To other peoples this may seem still not excessive, but the average annual income of the members for 1928, according to tax returns, was only £44. In addition, of course, the Credit Banks encourage deposits.

The great majority of the loans are granted on personal bond, but to some, and lately an increasing extent, mortgages are also issued. In 1925 a loan of £532,000 was received from the State, and from that and their own funds the banks have made considerable building advances, especially for land settlement. Strict control is exercised to see that the Raiffeisen principle is rigidly observed that loans are granted only for the furtherance of production. For this purpose special supervisors are appointed to visit borrowers and report on the use made of the money lent.

To what purpose, then, are these loans put? On this head 85 per cent. of the banks make returns to O.K.O., from which is learned that, in 1928, 600 new holdings were bought of 17,500 total acreage, and 50,000 acres were added to over 2,000 existing holdings. This new agriculture has been provided with buildings from the same source: over 3,000 dwellings and 11,000 other buildings have been erected. With similar assistance 27,000 acres of new land have been broken out, over 3,750 miles of new ditches have been dug, 12,000 farm animals have been bought, 126,000 sacks of manure, and 2,000,000 loads of top-dressing, besides large quantities of seed, feeding stuffs, and fodder.

Thus year by year strong and eager arms are helped by the Credit Banks to conquer new parishes of tilth from the waste, and in many other ways does this self-help-provided capital promote national and individual welfare and prosperity.

Deposits totalled £1,420,000 at the end of 1928, increasing during the year by £610,000 or 75 per cent. Share capital and deposits are supplemented by credit from O.K.O. During practically the whole existence of co-operative credit the State has placed funds at O.K.O.'s disposal, and has raised moneys for its use in other ways, even by borrowing abroad, so that at the end of 1928 the State was a creditor for £2,790,000.

O.K.O. also receives deposits and has discount privileges with Finland's National Bank. Re-discounts at the close of 1928 amounted to £455,000. The total advances to local banks were £3,720,000, of which £775,000 took the form of bills, £1,760,000 current credit, and £1,190,000 loans. Co-operative creameries, consumer co-operatives, etc., may also borrow of O.K.O. The accommodation to these "secondary" clients amounted at the same date to £212,000.

Careful Supervision of the Use of Credit

This extensive lending, based finally on personal credit, calls obviously for careful and expert supervision. Such supervision has been a leading feature of O.K.O. activities from its commencement, controlled by Professor Gebhard, as managing director. An organisation has been built up which provides continuous surveillance by capable, conscientious, and responsible auditors. O.K.O. employs seventeen district auditors—Pellervo's five consultants have passed through this grade—with three superintendents over these, and for more exacting audits and examinations of accounts.

A central Solvency Register is kept, in which are recorded details of the position and progress of all borrowers, whether local Credit Banks, co-operative creameries, or consumer co-operatives. Systematic training is provided for managers and book-keepers of Credit Banks in classes lasting usually three to four weeks. In addition, a large number of shorter courses of two or three days are arranged; in 1928 there were twenty-six, attended by 860 pupils. Correspondence tuition is also available.

In this educational work district organisations lend a hand: the local Associations of Credit Banks, of which 79 have been formed with 560 banks affiliated. A propaganda and education Central Union (Osuuskassojen Keskusliitto or O.K.) was formed in 1928, to which has now been assigned the audit work and staff training. The number of district auditors has recently been increased to twenty. O.K.O. and O.K. work in close collaboration, and to a large extent the management of both is in the same hands.

Credit Banks' Internal Problems

Thanks to all this deliberate training, the important problem of management of the banks is in a fair way of solution. Following Raiffeisen's suggestions, attempt was first made to interest the clergy in supervision and control, but without result. On the other hand, some hundreds of teachers keep accounts for the bank. By far the largest number of book-keepers are, however, farmers or farmers' sons or daughters. Office accommodation is often provided in the book-keeper's home, but communal offices, schools, etc., are also utilised. Several banks have their own premises, rarely very pretentious.

The daily work is very variously performed. Some banks open for business two or three days in the week. Others open every day, and serve as a kind of clearing house, through which, for example, members may be credited their local creamery payments, and settle with their consumer co-operative by order thereupon. On the other hand, there are banks that open only a few times in the month.

In all the management costs incredibly little. The total expenses of all the local banks for book-keepers' wages, executives' emoluments, etc., in 1927 did not exceed £23,700, an insignificant enough sum in relation to the total of advances, all in small amounts—over £3,600,000. The average of these expenses per bank per annum was £17.

In the few years of its existence the Co-operative Credit movement has been of enormous benefit to the agricultural population, especially those of slender means. In every sphere of their co-operative activity it has proved a valuable instrument for the promotion of responsible and intelligent self-help. It has now consolidated its position after the strain of the troubled years of crises, and bids fair in the time to come, and soon, to exceed the fondest hopes.

Building up reserves to give command of capital is the movement's main financial policy. Practically all O.K.O.'s surplus finds its way there—not merely the 50 per cent. directed by rule. The same is true of the local banks. Their own capital grows rapidly, and with the increase of deposits evident in recent years State assistance may become soon less necessary.

On the other hand, the State connection has been of mutual advantage. O.K.O. is indispensable to the full development of the co-operative Credit Banking movement, and the State has gained by the help and encouragement afforded to an industrious, ambitious, and thrifty smallholder class.

The complete and excellent manner in which the small man's needs are met is possible because the frugal poor invest their scanty savings in just the way that permits the satisfaction of that need. In 1928 there were £58,380,000 of deposits in the various banking institutions, of which £24,280,000 were lodged in private Savings Banks, Credit Banks, and O.K.O., in consumer co-operatives' savings departments, and in the Post Office Savings Bank.

The rapidly increasing importance of these small banks is shown by the fact that whereas, in 1920, 25 per cent. of all deposits were held by the latter, the small banks, their share is now 42 per cent. Finland's farmers and workers have learned the value of organisation and self-help in credit as in other directions. "Providence helps those who help themselves." This was the real import of the message that the young Gebhard brought his countrymen thirty years ago.

CHAPTER IX

CO-OPERATIVE CREAMERIES AND OTHER PRODUCTIVE UNDERTAKINGS

In 1260 the peasants of Finland, as the chronicles relate, paid part of their taxes in butter; and in 1560 butter was exported from Finland to Danzig, Lubeck, Denmark, and Holland, and formed half the country's exports.

The milk trade of Finland has thus very venerable traditions. The Finnish word for cow, "lehmä", is old Finnish, deriving from the time when the early Finn-Magyar race roamed the Volga banks; and that for cattle, "nauta", is a Nordic loan-word from the beginning of our era or perhaps even earlier.

For modern Finland the milk trade has extraordinary importance, since half of the country's farmland is devoted to dairy farming, and milk products, butter, and cheese take second place in export tables, inferior only to timber and timber goods. The burden of this trade is carried by the little polled Finnish cow, light red in West Finland, white and red in Eastern districts. Typical of the country, tough and hardy, little susceptible to disease, particularly immune from tuberculosis, it thrives on the scrub and moorland, repays feeding, and yields well considering its size, and its milk is remarkably rich in butter-fat. Great attention has been paid to improvement of the breed, especially since 1898, and cattle-breeding societies do excellent work with shows, awards, and selection in other ways of pedigreed bulls.

The co-operative movement is a valuable factor even at this stage, promoting production through bull and control societies, both dating back to the end of last century. While not fully or precisely co-operative, these associations generally accompany co-operative agricultural development, and certainly thrive best in such company. The latest figures give 170 bull societies, and 729 control societies extending to 203,500 cows. Since 1918 control societies have increased by 576, and in the interval the milk yield per cow has increased without interruption, both absolutely and per feed unit.

The average yield for 1926–7 was 5,635 lb., against 3,496 in 1918, and per 100 feed units has risen from 271 to 288. The average butter-fat content runs as high as 3·94 per cent. The work of the control societies has thus been most effective, but, as yet, only 15·8 per cent. of the whole cow population is enrolled in these societies. In comparison the figures for Sweden are 647 societies with 215,000 cows, a milk production of 7,407 lb., and an average fat content of 3·57 per cent. The Finnish cow gives less milk but richer; it is especially a "butter" cow that the breeding societies have managed to rear during these years. One of the best West Finland cows in 1926 milked over 19,800 lb., with 838 lb. of butter-fat.

The number of cows in Finland is very large in proportion to population: about 35 per 100 inhabitants. Milk, butter, and cheese are consumed at home to a much larger extent than in other countries. As stated in the opening chapter, the amount of margarine eaten per head is no more than 6½ lb. per annum, In country districts this modern substitute is little known; the fat requirements of the people—far from light, especially in the bitter winter and in the strenuous lumbering and timber-driving, which is usually left until the frozen snow provides natural roadways—are met almost wholly by butter.

Should the margarine habit take, the butter export, 18,000 tons in 1928, will rapidly expand. The remarkable development of that export, especially since the war, and the high esteem in which Finnish milk products are held, are almost entirely to be ascribed to the very efficiently organised co-operative creamery movement, and the energy and ability of its central export association, Valio, with its counterpart among the Swedish-speaking, Enigheten (Unity).

The Rise of Modern Dairying

As late as seventy years ago dairying in Finland was still very primitive; cows roamed the moors and marshes, winter feeding was meagre—little but rye-straw—and the summer butter, heavily salted, was kept till autumn and sold to travelling buyers, who packed it in big wooden cases and sent it to Russia and Germany.

Then whitewood barrels were introduced, but still Finnish butter was considered a low-grade article on the world market. In the sixties, however, some of the large estates engaged experienced dairymen from Holstein, whose new methods soon found general favour. Crop failures in the late sixties accelerated the farming transition from grain to cattle. The big-estate creameries became in time purchasing creameries; their plant and staffs could be more fully and therefore more economically utilised when neighbouring farmers were persuaded to sell and send their milk.

Before long the milk received from outside exceeded that produced by the creamery owners, and creameries came into existence that bought all the milk they manufactured, producing none themselves. In their heyday, 1885–95, there are reckoned to have been at least 1,500 such creameries. Both production and export went up by leaps and bounds, but the weakness of the system made itself manifest. The creameries paid no attention to butter-fat content, so water adulteration crept in. The object of the creameries being simply the maximum of profit to their proprietors, these resorted to squeezing their suppliers. Quantity not quality became their aim, and training of staff and maintenance of plant went unheeded.

Eventually the Joint Stock Creamery took the field, an instinctive gesture in the direction of co-operation, on realisation of the defects of the purchasing creamery. Every shareholder subscribed capital in proportion to the number of his cows, and profit distribution therefore bore some rough indirect relation to the amount of milk supplied.

The joint-stock creameries diligently sought out experts, installed modern machinery, and studied quality. Many, however, soon degenerated into mere purchasing associations of the older type, the larger stockholders buying out the smaller, and distributing profits on capital which ceased to bear any relation to the shareholder's byre.

This type flourished from 1895 to 1902. In its first years butter production and export still continued to increase, the latter reaching 14,500 tons in 1897. The tendency to regress into purchasing factories, already noted, proved finally the undoing of the joint-stock creamery.

Co-operation to the Rescue!

About the end of the century, Hannes Gebhard began sounding the co-operative tocsin in the dairy farmers' ears, and Pellervo initiated the co-operative creamery movement. This took root forthwith in Finland, and in form and organisation has changed little since its introduction. The co-operative creameries are owned by their milk suppliers in common, every member contributing to the costs of erection, maintenance, and business, in precise proportion as he utilises the services of the creamery, and participating in any trading surplus in exact proportion to his milk supplies.

Any milk producer may join—Co-operation's Open Door—and every member has the same rights and responsibilities. Since the stream of new members never fails and may not be restrained, the creamery is, and must remain, its milk suppliers' own property, and all the mischief of profit-hunting at the cost of others completely and immediately disappears.

In the ultimate real interests of the members, the co-operative creamery movement in Finland, as elsewhere, has ever strenuously endeavoured to improve the quality of milk and milk products.

The rapid and even progress achieved is here depicted:

CO-OPERATIVE CREAMERY STATISTICS

Year.	Creameries.	Members.	Value of Sales, in £1,000.
1903	55	4,025	—
1905	168	15,801	420
1910	285	30,058	1,000
1915	381	41,380	1,500
1920	345	41,639	2,570
1925	602	57,769	3,605
1926	563	62,294	3,644
1927	664	68,092	4,358

In 1927 the cows owned by co-operative creamery members numbered 417,928, or just over 6 per member. The creameries are often small; the average membership, as shown above, is little over 100, and naturally increase in this respect is keenly sought with a view to increasing the creamery's business and so keeping down expenses per cwt. of butter.

But in Finland distances and transport conditions impose harsh and definite limits on concentration. The co-operative creamery becomes of necessity a village or parish undertaking. This is not without advantage in that there is closer community among the members, all personally known to each other, and the more frequent contact and better acquaintance constitutes in itself a mild but fairly effective form of control. Few creameries, and those principally in the north and east, cover territory so large that they need collecting stations for their milk.

From the average number of cows per member is at once evident that the members are very largely in a small way of farming. But large farmers and landed proprietors have often found membership to their advantage also. Calculations give that some 40 per cent. of the members own each not more than 3 cows, 55 per cent. 4 to 15, and the remainder more than 15.

The total number of cows attached to co-operative creameries is one-third of the whole number in the country, which means that the big majority of the cows producing milk for sale support the co-operatives. Naturally the numerous cottars, smallholders, country residents, artisans, and labourers, who own only one or two cows for their domestic supplies, have no interest in membership of a co-operative creamery; nor have those larger farms and estates who for years have had creameries of their own, and whose herds are large enough to make such creameries pay.

Thus the co-operative creamery is the absolutely dominant form throughout Finland. In 1927 more than 80 per cent. of all in the country were co-operative, and of the total calculated creamery butter production—22,300 tons—21,000 represents the co-operative share. In little more than a quarter of a century co-operation has wrought a peaceful revolution and captured Finland's dairy business.

Creamery Organisation and Finance

Of 625 creameries reporting in 1928, 111 are co-operatives without any but share obligations on the member,

388 have a limited further liability, and 126 unlimited liability. All have adopted Pellervo model rules with little modification, and a uniformity of constitution and method has resulted which has considerably facilitated amalgamation.

Under these rules every member must subscribe one share of approximately £1 for every milk-cow he owns, and must, if required, advance to the creamery a loan not exceeding 1½ times his share liability. Only 1s. of each share needs to be paid down; the balance is deducted in instalments from milk payments. The price paid is determined monthly on a butter-fat basis, and according to the price received for milk products. From receipts there fall to be deducted 5 to 18 per cent., as computed by the executive, for wages and other direct charges; 3 per cent. for maintenance, repairs, extensions, and sinking fund; 1 per cent. to reserves; 2 per cent. to payment of balance of members' shares, and 2 per cent. to the supplementary loan that members have to contribute.

The explanation of these supplementary loans is that when the original model rules were drafted fear was felt that, if the share subscription was set too high, the creameries' capital might become excessive, since share capital was not repayable except on retiral from membership. So the share was fixed comparatively low, and the optional supplementary loan was introduced, similarly non-withdrawable, but repayable at the management's option, so that capital might be adjusted to meet requirements. Unfortunately the spate of share capital failed to materialise, and now the supplementary loan is giving way to a higher rate of share subscription.

The co-operative creamery is based on the compulsory delivery of all the milk of each member, with heavy penalties for infraction. Only sufficient for household requirements may be retained, and membership may not be relinquished during its first two years. A member leaving within five years forfeits his share in the supplementary loan, and leaving after five years and within ten years of his admission he forfeits half thereof.

Usually no great pressure is needed to persuade members to fulfil their contract; the smallness of the society ensures that withholding or diverting of milk cannot well be concealed, and a quiet hint from neighbours and friends is usually enough to recall the transgressor to rectitude.

The rules direct that one-fourth of the surplus be carried to reserve, until this amounts to £258. The balance, after payment of interest on shares, is submitted to the Annual General Meeting for disposal. Reserve funds suffered severely from the inflation of wartime and the following years, but in most of the creameries this ravage is being rapidly repaired. In 1927, 513 co-operatives investigated provided from their own resources 45 per cent. of their working capital. Shares, supplementary loans, reserves, and sinking and other such funds amounted in all to £438,000, while the remainder consisted of £126,000 State loans and £444,000 bank and private loans. Losses for 1926 ran only to £5,800. So the need for reserving is equally met in the rules and in practice.

Management control is vested in the Annual General Meeting assembling twice a year, before the end of March and October, and the Executive which meets once a month or oftener at need. The Executive members receive a certain modest emolument, but are not full-time officials. The daily current management is in the hands of a foreman or manager, who may not be a member of the Executive, the idea being to restrict the influence of the manager in the government of the society. Final decision rests with the members in all matters, but in practice any keen, competent, straightforward manager, and thanks to the creamery schools and the relatively high standard of staff training, this type is now the rule, gets all the authority or scope he needs to manage the creamery on expert lines and in the most economical manner.

So far as capital resources permit, the rules allow creameries to extend into other related lines of business. Thus encouraged, many own piggeries, to make the most remunerative use of their skim-milk. Some own saw-mills, others flour-mills, and a number both. The motive here has plainly been to establish the creamery and its adjuncts as a centre of general common production and power storage. At the end of 1927 there were 56 with piggeries, 52 with flour-mills, 22 with saw-mills, and 16 with other secondary industries. These combination creameries are more exacting in their demands on managerial ability and versatility, but many of them have flattering results to show.

Hallmark: Quality

This rapid progress has been possible in Finland because special stress has always been laid on quality and organised selling. A long road has been travelled since the Finn and Russian butter-buyers in Karelen soaked their wooden scales every night in brine so that they might swindle the poor seller out of extra weight. In modern creameries, and especially in co-operative creameries, owned as they are by the members themselves, such tricks and meanness are inconceivable, and the ceaseless efforts of Valio to educate members to the supreme value of high milk quality have brought the farmer and his house enormous gain in the material form of successive increases in the price of milk. The quality attained enables Valio to dare world markets with their butter and cheese, and there to get ever higher prices, which in due course enable the creameries to pay their members still more for their milk.

Since 1921, or rather, perhaps, since 1910–11, payment for milk on a quality, as well as a fat, basis has been vigorously advocated, and with such success that this is now the rule in all that make butter for export—by far the largest number.

The milk is examined both as to cleanliness and purity and as to its fat content. Gerber's acid method is in general use for fat determination and Barthel-Orla-Jensen's for quality, and payment is made on fat-content basis with a deduction or premium for quality.

Cream is bought on a similar basis at those creameries which because of the remoteness of supplies and transport difficulties receive their raw material in that form. All the milk used in butter manufacture is pasteurised. To the improvement of milk the District Creamery Associations have made sterling contribution. Years ago they started milk judging for prizes; they arrange butter and cheese shows, give expert advice, and run competitions of various kinds to stimulate the interest of employees in their work. Altogether there are 14 District Creamery Associations—11 in the Finnish-speaking areas, 3 in Swedish-speaking.

The success of these efforts will be appreciated from the fact that 85 per cent. of all affiliated creameries now tangibly recognise quality; in one association, in South-West Finland, the percentage is actually 100. Not only milk for butter manufacture is paid on this basis, but that for direct consumption as well.

Besides the butter and cheese creameries there are milk-selling societies vending liquid milk to the home consumer, or supplying shops in towns and industrial centres. These also are extremely well managed and subject to thorough supervision. They in turn are associated in districts.

Valio handles 90 per cent. of Co-operative Creamery Butter

Finnish butter and cheese would certainly not have been able in so short a time to rank alongside those of Denmark, Holland, Sweden, Switzerland, etc., had the co-operative creameries relied on selling their export produce through private firms. As is generally well-known, the reputation of a foreign commodity, by which of course its price is regulated, is extremely sensitive, and depends not on any average merit, but on the worst consignments on offer, no matter how few or small. A single firm, greedy for profit, needs only to water down the butter, or to re-churn or blend it with inferior or stale, for the whole article to fall into evil repute, however long hitherto it may have been above reproach, or even unequalled.

With this well in mind, therefore, the co-operative creameries in 1905 set up their own central export agency, Valio, meaning "select". To-day 90 per cent. of all Finnish butter exported is sold through Valio. As its Swedish compeer, Enigheten, sells about 6 per cent., poor pickings—no more than 4 per cent.—remain for the private firms. Less progress has been made in regard to cheese, but, even so, Valio is far the largest exporter of Finnish cheese, and 50 per cent. of all the country's cheese exports comes from Valio's creameries.

Valio handles Greater Part of Home Milk Supply to Towns

Valio's activities are many and mixed; but its original purpose still holds pride of place. Beginning with seventeen co-operative creameries, and an annual production of 900 tons of butter, in 1928 it reached 15,350 tons, of which 11,850 were exported. A highly ramified and successful international butter sale has been organised; suitable storage and transport have been made possible by assembly of produce, and a number of special creameries have been erected to assist in regulating supplies to demand, and so to maintain the price.

For if demand and, following, the price suddenly rise in one town, milk flows there, and local creameries may be left minus. Should world prices of butter and cheese begin to soar, there may be milk shortage in industrial areas in the homeland. Such fluctuations are harmful to trade, disturb the even course of development, and injure sales. Regulation benefits even the consumer, ensuring him constant supplies. Recently Valio has built large modern milk-sales depots in Helsingfors, Tammerfors, Viborg, and an old, somewhat out-of-date creamery in Åbo is to be reconstructed. In several of these towns Valio also retails, but not in Helsingfors, where Elanto, with others, attends to that.

Valio's creameries are equipped for the production of butter, cheese, condensed milk, and casein, so as to utilise surplus during the milk-flood period, which, strangely enough, in Finland occurs rather in winter and early spring than in summer, the result of the enormous attention bestowed on fodder-growing and byre-feeding. Now Valio, as will be seen, has taken in hand pasture improvement so as to increase summer production too.

These special creameries serve excellent purpose as models. There Valio's cheese experts are employed, engaged from famous cheese countries, and the latest machinery and methods are put to the test. Thence is spread through Finland knowledge of the art of manufacturing good Gruyère cheese; at present Edam is receiving special notice under the guidance of one of Holland's cleverest makers. An object-lesson is provided to school and class of how a modern creamery should be arranged and managed.

In 1928 the total receipts of Valio creameries were 12,000,000 gallons of milk and 750 tons of butter, and large quantities of cheese were manufactured. Spacious and modern storage is attached for butter and cheese from affiliated creameries, mostly for the home market, and for use as intermediate stations for butter on its way overseas from the producer, with first-class chill and ventilation arrangements, and with accommodation for 800 tons of butter and 8,000 large Gruyère cheeses.

Masterly Organisation of Butter Export

The manner in which Valio has organised the butter and cheese trade of Finland is most admirable, and may well serve as fitting example for any country. Results have been highly gratifying; in the first five years Valio reduced the margin between its average price and the average of Copenhagen quotations from 14s. 6d. to 4s. 4d., and in 1928 Finnish butter was quoted on the average in Manchester at 184s. per cwt. against 183s. 11d. for Swedish and 190s. 7d. for Danish. In 1926 Danish was 9s. 2d. above Finnish; 1928 saw the difference cut to 6s. 7d. The two great actuating principles that have made such progress possible have been consistent payment on quality for cheese and butter to all affiliated creameries and the sleepless vigilance with which every consignment is examined that goes abroad in Valio's name.

Propaganda for quality payment was begun by Valio long before the State had thought of troubling itself with control of butter export. But from 1913 State control became operative. In essentials the State simply follows where Valio led; and it was with Valio's help and guidance that the State Agricultural Department was able to devise a scheme of compulsory supervision over all export butter.

Valio, however, controls, equally effectively, all butter for home sale, for, since 1921, all receives a bonus according to its official quality grading, and in recent years, to spur the emulation of creameries and their staffs, annual quality competitions are held where prizes and diplomas are awarded. For butter, the State quality standards and tests are adopted.

From the beginning of 1929 the State Butter Control station took over also the control of cheese, and, as with butter, graded bonus is paid by the exporter for quality, which naturally encourages excellence of production. No less than 85 per cent. of the Gruyère cheese made is now high-class export cheese, finding market sometimes even in Holland. The cleverest makers gain prizes and diplomas, as do the butter-makers, at the annual shows. In particular, the special prizes awarded to those butter-makers and cheese-makers who for three successive years achieve the best average results, are greatly coveted and excite keen competition.

Butter Control in Operation

On certain days of the week, usually Mondays, the special butter trains, with their well-known white refrigerator vans, arrive in Hangö, the principal export harbour and the State's principal control station. During the winter ice is cut and stored at certain junctions, and here in warmer weather the refrigerator vans are replenished.

When Hangö is frozen up, which rarely happens, export goes through Åbo. The trains are unloaded and the consignments sorted out in a large hall. Thence they go into separate storage. Samples are taken from each parcel, and examined by three experts for odour, taste, and quality. Each allots his points independently and gives his verdict; the points and opinions are then averaged.

Every detail is observed down to the appearance of the casks, packing, etc. At the same time, samples are taken for test of water content, genuineness, etc. In addition, four times a year, without notice of any kind, further samples are taken from every creamery's butter, classified, and then preserved for fourteen days, and judged anew, to determine keeping merit. The results are later communicated with the weekly reports.

On Tuesday the exporters learn the results, the butter goes on board ship and sails on Wednesday for Hull, Stettin, and elsewhere. The following Monday it appears on the consumer's table, and as usually a week at most elapses between despatch from the creameries and arrival at Hangö, a fortnight suffices to carry it from churn to loaf. This has only been possible through the highly efficient collecting organisation created by Valio.

Two weeks after receipt of the butter, Valio remits to the creameries, whether sale has been effected or not. Price is calculated on the basis of market conditions on the day of receipt. Remittance for cheese is made monthly. Should the price determined prove too low, additional payment is made at the end of the year or earlier, if desired. If too high, Valio itself bears the loss.

Generally, however, a margin is allowed to cover expenses, possible loss through fluctuations of the market prices, and some small surplus, which usually goes to reserve. According to rule, 20 per cent. of any surplus resulting is to be carried to contingency or reserve funds. The remainder goes to pay interest on share capital, seriously diminished by inflation, and towards the improvement of creamery practice and of pasturage and agriculture generally. Affiliated creameries are under contract to deliver to Valio the whole of their manufacture.

The rapid rise of Valio is well illustrated in the following table:

Year.	Number of Creameries Affiliated.	Total Sales, in £1,000.	Total Reserves, in £1,000.
1905	34	—	2·4
1910	157	532	16
1915	251	1,130	41
1920	295	1,880	62
1925	405	3,130	73
1926	438	3,015	84
1927	462	3,393	94
1928	485	3,406	105

Valio and Creamery Development and Pasturage Improvement

Fitting complement to Valio's business activities is shown in its scientific and propaganda work. Quite early in the co-operative creamery movement the necessity obtruded for attention to increase of milk products. The justly famous central laboratory of Valio has for chief one of Finland's best-known chemists, Dr. Artturi Virtanen, and employs besides seven trained chemists and bacteriologists, with a small army of assistants. Pure cultures are grown of cheese bacteria, bacteria active in the acidification of cream and of nitrogen-gathering bacteria, which are supplied to farmers. With the help of these the nitrogen content of the soil, and thus its fertility, can be substantially increased.

Other investigations are conducted of general importance for creameries in cattle management and agriculture—for example, on butter bacteria and their value to keeping quality, cheese ripening and aeration, and cheese bacteria culture. In 1928 the laboratory published no fewer than ten scientific researches: six in Finnish, three in German, and one in English. The laboratory examines, of course, Valio's own products also and materials used in creameries: oils, salt, butter-colouring, etc. In the words of one of Valio's directors: "The many extensive bacteriological investigations made in Valio laboratory in recent years will as time passes prove, we are convinced, epoch-making in the development of the dairy industry in Finland."

Much is done to promote creamery instruction. Valio has its own institute for the training of teachers and managers, and organises classes in different areas in creamery management. A building and technical department has been established which designs and builds and advises on machinery, etc. Business consultation is also available, and pasturage improvement is now the subject of much experiment. For this purpose Valio employs eleven working foremen, one for each creamery association's district and two for milk-selling districts, superintended by a special pasturage consultant. With this assistance practical demonstrations have been held, at which some 7,500 acres have been submitted to public treatment.

Valio also compiles and publishes trade statistics for the Finnish co-operative creameries. Public propaganda and education are purveyed by periodicals: *Karjatalous* (*Cattle Management*) and *Karjantuote* (*Cattle Breeding*). The first has an edition of 52,000 and reaches the most of co-operative creamery members; the second has 3,000 subscribers. Many excellent text-books, in Finnish, are also published.

The manner in which Valio has been built up agrees in the main with that which has characterised other co-operative central organisations. The Annual General Meeting elects a Supervisory Council of fifteen, which in turn appoints a Managing Executive of three. The division of duties tallies essentially with that which obtains, for example, in Hankkija.

Valio's Story

"The story of Valio's development", says the same director in a bright little pamphlet on Finland's creameries, "may well be compared with the account by the prophet Nehemiah of the building of the walls of Jerusalem. Just as Tobiah, the Ammonite, scornfully declared to Sanballat, the Horonite, that the new walls would crumble if but a fox should leap upon them, so did our private butter exporters deride the idea of a co-operative association for butter export, and assert that the impudent young Valio must collapse of its own ineptitude. And just as the enemies about Jerusalem joined forces to fight the children of Israel, so did the private butter exporters league together to wage war against Valio. Therefore Valio has had to fight as did the children of Israel—with the sword in one hand and the trowel in the other."

The passing years have seen a magnificent structure grow up in this way. The universal opinion now in Finland is that the co-operative creamery had never become what it is, had never accomplished what it has accomplished, without its energetic and resourceful trading central, Valio. Valio's work has cheapened selling itself and has raised the quality of produce enormously; but its services far exceed that: it has inspired the tillers of the soil with a due sense of their own importance and a proud confidence in their own strength, enabling them with calm and bold assurance to attempt and to effect themselves the improvement of their own business, their own acres.

Enigheten and its Work

This second creamery union carries on the tale of Valio's exploits, and on much the same lines. Small by comparison with Valio, it is yet much larger than any of the private butter exporters. To Enigheten are affiliated a score of co-operative creameries in the Swedish-speaking areas, principally in Österbotten; headquarters are in Helsingfors. These too insist strictly on quality, which they also encourage by graded bonus.

As already stated, three of the Creamery District Associations lie in this territory. Intimate relations exist between them and Enigheten, which accords the Associations pecuniary support, amply repaid by their keen interest in quality propaganda and creamery training. Enigheten maintains Finland's only Swedish-speaking creamery college, in Gamlakarleby, arranges butter shows, supplies advice, etc.

The District Associations and the college are further helped by publications, which include a creamery textbook and a periodical—*Enigheten*, in Swedish. 1928 turnover was £222,000, of which £191,000 represented butter to the weight of 1,100 tons. The government is similar to Valio's.

As Enigheten exports 6 per cent. of all Finland's butter export and 14·2 per cent. of all its cheese, no less than 96 per cent. of all butter exported and 64 per cent. of all cheese come from the two co-operative central organisations—truly a magnificent achievement in so short a time! Little remains of present butter production to capture, but there is every prospect of much expansion even there, and positive certainty as regards cheese.

Co-operative Slaughter-houses and Cattle Wholesale

The statistics of co-operative slaughter-house societies seem trivial following those just reviewed. Their present number is eight, with some 5,000 individual members and thirty group members. Sales total 5,500 tons of meat of the value of £517,000, and the number of slaughtering establishments is fifteen, including four for export, with ten sausage and meat factories, and several other productive works. A number of cattle-sale societies, co-operate creameries, and milk societies have combined to form a central organisation.

This organisation, S.K. or Suomen Karjakeskuskunta (Finland's Central Cattle Society), functions in a mixed capacity in that it operates both as a control organisation, and as a local society. Wholesale meat businesses have been set up in Helsingfors, where S.K. has an up-to-date meat factory. A very modern warehouse and factory have been erected at Viborg. In 1922 an export slaughter-house was built in Torneå for the Swedish export trade, in which S.K. figured largely, until an increased Swedish tariff proved prohibitive. The meat exported is obtained partly from the members, partly on the open market. The affiliated slaughter-houses sell exclusively to S.K. The total turnover in the first year of operations, 1919, was £210,000, by 1923 it had exceeded £290,000, reaching £377,000, in 1926, and, in 1928, £512,000, representing 4,900 tons of meat.

In Viborg and Helsingfors, S.K. has some thirty retail shops, several of the highest class.

Reorganisation of the co-operative meat trade is at present under consideration, with proposals to improve and standardise supplies, and to delimit producer and consumer fields of operation. The trade is mainly in beef; very little bacon is eaten and none is exported. Meantime, activities are confined principally to local domestic markets.

Egg-sale Societies and their Central

Finnish egg-sale societies have also their central, of the Valio type: Vientikunta Muna—whose aim is, by Valio methods, as far as suitable, to secure more even and improved quality of export eggs. Collecting stations receive the eggs for forwarding through Helsingfors and Åbo to England, Sweden, and other countries.

In 1929 there were 152 egg societies, with approximate membership of 10,000, affiliated to Muna. Turnover value is as yet comparatively small, but affiliation has steadily increased since the agency was started in 1921; sales in 1928 amounted to £37,200, an increase on 1927 of £27,400. Headquarters are in Helsingfors.

Timber-sale Societies and their Central

These too have now their central organisation: Metsänomistajain Metsäkuskus, or M.M., ages with Muna, but with, naturally, much larger turnover, reaching £455,000, mainly export. M.M. owns quays, timber-yards, and shipping in a number of centres. The largest, at Makslahti, is intended, when complete, to have loading facilities for 15,000 to 20,000 standards a year.

M.M. takes the form of a joint-stock company, its shareholders being timber-sale societies and lumbering associations in various parts of the country. These at the close of 1928 number in all ten, with about 4,500 members, and supply sawed timber from their own or rented saw-mills.

Other Productive Societies

Other co-operatives, such as those concerned with machinery, moss-litter, saw-milling, flour-milling, electrical power distribution, telephones, have no central organisations. They feel less need thereof than co-operative creameries, Credit Banks, etc.

Machinery and moss-litter co-operatives are very

numerous. The special function of the former is the purchase of such plant as threshing mills for common use; they handle now tractors, motors, reapers, self-binders, sowing machines, etc., and even larger and costlier agricultural machinery; in number they count 450, with around 4,500 members.

The machines acquired are hired out to members, and any surplus is divided in proportion to the number of hours hired. Losses are not unknown unfortunately, and the societies labour under peculiar difficulties. On the other hand, they have been of great service, providing machinery for many smallholders and farmers who could never hope otherwise to benefit by its labour-saving. Indeed, old-fashioned flail-threshing has practically been abolished by these societies.

Several are financed by Co-operative Credit Banks.

The same remarks apply to moss-litter societies, numbering 165, with 4,700 members, and turning out £28,000 worth in the year. These have a propaganda value of their own in that they have very largely converted farmers from the use of poor, bad straw for animal bedding to the more hygienic moss-litter.

Remote and lonely parishes are cheered and brightened now with telephone and electricity supplied by co-operatives, and a very necessary forward impulse has thus been imparted. Of telephone societies there are 250 with 12,800 members and an annual turnover of £32,000.

There are registered 190 distributive electrical societies with 9,000 members and a total trade of £150,000 in the year. While some provide lighting only, others power small saw-mills or flour-mills.

Bull and other pedigree societies have already been noticed. Their importance belongs rather to the creamery section. Several of them have finished the year at times with a deficit, but assistance has invariably been forthcoming from Co-operative Credit Banks and co-operative creameries. In 1928 there were in all 380 societies of this type, having 5,200 members.

Housing societies have already been mentioned. In recent years several co-operative associations have been formed for autobus service and for steamer traffic on some of Finland's 35,500 lakes.

CHAPTER X

CO-OPERATIVE INSURANCE

Relatively the youngest, but far from the least of co-operative activities in Finland is the insurance movement. By many this is considered one of the branches of Finnish co-operation with the greatest possibilities, since insurance in Finland is certainly highly developed in technique and in organisation, while the insurance habit among the people is still far from as general as in other countries.

This is to be expected from the low standard of living so long obtaining in Finland, and from the upheavals in and after the war that so impoverished her. Slowly but surely capital again accumulates, and thereby co-operative insurance is seen to have an important part to play. In fire and life assurance first rank is already in sight, even though the private businesses, mostly senior to the co-operative, as a whole dominate and include the very largest life and fire companies.

S.O.K. Insurance

A start was made in fire insurance—Tulenvara—over twenty years ago by S.O.K., which now insures the property of societies and members to the value of £7,209,000. Shareholder societies number 606 and policies 16,720. The funds amount to £192,000, of which, however, the Guarantee Fund of £172,000 consists of members' supplementary shares' subscriptions in the shape of promissory notes. In 1918 an Insurance Pension Scheme—Elonvara ("Support of Old Age")—was instituted for the staffs of S.O.K. and affiliated societies, to cover death, sickness, disablement, and old age. This was supplemented in 1919 by Työväenturva ("Support of the Workers"), later renamed Oma ("Our Own"), providing Workmen's Compensation.

But the largest and most important of S.O.K. insurance efforts is the life assurance society Pohja (The North). Young in years, founded only in 1923, it has leaped into popularity and success. In its first six years policies in force increased in number from 7,600 to 75,000, the amount insured from £507,000 to £3,559,000, and the premium reserve from £8,300 to £158,700.

The Society has a large number of agents all over the country, and consumer co-operative managers and executives of co-operative creameries and Credit Banks actively push its business. The insurers are generally smallholders and peasants, as is evident from the average size of policy, around £79, which proves that Pohja is a real people's insurance society. The government consists of a Supervisory Council of twelve and an Executive of four.

K.K. Insurance

Insurance business in K.K. circles is concentrated in two undertakings: Kansa (The People) Life and Kansa Fire, the latter the older. This was established in 1919, and was originally a department of OTK managed along with OTK's savings department. Immediately the mark began to stabilise life assurance was urged, and K.K. Congress in 1923 decided to begin therewith.

The first life policy was issued October 1, 1923. Though, nominally, two separate departments, and accounting separately, Kansa Fire and Kansa Life have the same executive and the same headquarters and are practically one.

The number of life policies has increased with the years from 2,300 to 70,000, and the total sum assured from £71,000 to £3,799,000. The average in Kansa Life is less than in Pohja, or about £48; the insurers are largely of the working class. Group insurance is also undertaken for the staffs of societies. The premium can by grouping be kept very low, or about 1 per cent. of wages, because only death is covered. About three-fourths of the employees in the K.K. movement are so insured. Most societies insure at £26 per head, rising often after five years' service to double that sum. The total assured under this head in 1929 was £174,000.

Kansa Life has, further, concentrated within itself the burial funds of K.K. societies. Many of these funds paid burial money to the relatives of deceased members who in their last year had purchased up to a certain amount. Centralisation of this assistance in Kansa was found to be of advantage. The total ultimate liability under this head in 1929 was £232,000 and the number insured 90,000.

Kansa Life has, lastly, an Accident Insurance to meet the requirements of the new Finnish Accident Insurance Act, which includes shop staffs within its scope. To retain all co-operative insurance in co-operative hands, Kansa Life deemed it advisable to cater also for this compulsory provision. Smaller private employers have also joined Kansa for this purpose. On the other hand, this Society engages only to a very small extent in collective accident insurance.

In ten years Kansa Fire has increased its policies from 1,113 to 33,700, and the sum assured from £579,000 to £8,466,000. The clientèle consists principally of societies and their members.

Both Life and Fire branches have accumulated large funds. On December 31, 1929, Kansa Life had £76,700 reserves and £189,300 premium reserve, while Kansa Fire had funds amounting to £185,900. The managing executive consists of five members.

The inspiring progress of Finland's co-operative insurance is well illustrated in the fact that Kansa and Pohja together in 1929 issued 29,000 new policies of in all, £1,873,000, or nearly one-fourth of the total new insurance for the year and more than one-fourth of the new policies. In property insurance not much beyond a good beginning has been made, but the present rate of advance promises that before long this branch of insurance will also take high rank in Finnish co-operation.

As already explained, while not allowed legal co-operative form, these mutual insurance societies are fully co-operative in method and effect.

Insurance, in one form or another, is an ancient practice in Finland. For many generations the fire risks of the parish, or, sometimes, of several parishes, have been pooled. In 1927 there were 293 of these local institutions, operating now largely under rules prepared for them by Pellervo, which also, in 1917, helped them to form a Reinsurance Society—Vakava—in fuller cover of their risks. This organisation, with 144 societies in membership in 1929, £16,300 of funds, and £12,900,000 of reinsurance, further assists its affiliated societies with business advice, and encourages the development of fire-extinguishing apparatus and fire-prevention devices.

In 1904 Pellervo devised model rules, and issued a handbook for live-stock insurance companies then finding favour. With this impetus their number increased to 129 in 1916, but the Great War and its sequel had disastrous effects, so that the number fell to 92 in 1926.

Again Pellervo came to their aid, and in 1926 a Live-Stock Reinsurance Society—Kekri—was formed. Though the number of member societies is only 24, the insurance represented is now approximately one-fifth of the live-stock insurance of the whole country.

Owners of growing timber have also their own insurance scheme, and the Aura Mutual Society insures against accidents in the agricultural world.

Valio and Hankkija each carry pension funds for the employees of their associate societies.

The origins of mutual aid trace back among the farming population to a remote and distant past, and so, largely, is explained the ready acceptance and understanding that modern co-operation has found.

CHAPTER XI

IN CONCLUSION

JUHANI. "Seven sons! Seven mouths to feed! What luck! Man and an unkind fate are leagued against us. . . ."
TUOMAS. "But hope is not yet dead."
JUHANI. " . . . Ilvesjärvi, beneath the slopes of Impivaara, shall be our refuge from the storm. I have spoken!"
TUOMAS. " . . . On we go! Together!"
JUHANI. "There we shall start the world anew."

This passage, that seems very appropriately to set off a final chapter on Finnish Co-operation, and to be a pleasant change from the contemplation of serried ranks of figures, is drawn from the modern national epic, *The Seven Brothers*, by Alexis Kivi. No wild resolve to revolutionise the world is implied in the common determination, but simply a decision to leave the paternal roof and acres that have become too narrow and few, to break out new land, to build a new home. With quiet courage they set out for Ilvesjärvi, where soon they have cleared the brush, ploughed and harrowed with seven-man power, to see in summer long waves of swelling grain ripple over the former waste. The bold decision, the venture into the new and unknown, the common toil, had been amply repaid. Despite differing temperaments and dispositions, the seven held together through fair and foul, and the author leaves them finally happy and content to teach what they have learned and to continue their conquest of the soil.

Much the same swift decision and intrepidity characterise the Finnish Co-operative movement, much the same common sympathy in trial and difficulty. They are faced with a like stern need of all hands to the plough to turn the furrows out of which Finland's prosperity shall shoot and grow. The co-operative movement has been the cement that held Finland together in the last generation of difficulty and strife. Progress has been made on different fronts, but not in enmity, in emulative struggle for the commonweal, and so Finnish co-operation impresses both with its great variety and with its accumulated and united power. The hopes of its founders have been realised so far that it has proved the means they sought for raising Finland materially and spiritually, for enabling the individual to improve his circumstances, increase the results of his labours, and so to broaden his views on life and participate ever more and more in the fruits of cultural progress, of common wisdom and knowledge.

Even a brief acquaintance leaves a vivid impression of the practical experience that the co-operative movement finds in various directions in Finland, and of the high importance it has attained in the material life of the nation. The grip that co-operation has is scarcely credible to outsiders. No question longer is raised over the superiority and benefit of the co-operative form of undertaking. It is accepted with the liveliest interest and greatest good will in all departments of public life, and in the Press of almost every hue from diehard Tory to rabid Communist. Most of Finnish adults belong to one or more co-operative organisations, and the local and personal benefits reaped have taught effectively the value of the movement as a whole.

A sound and thorough knowledge of the real nature of co-operation is far more general than perhaps in any other country. Deliberate and wilful misrepresentation of the kind so common elsewhere is almost inconceivable here. Co-operative results and success have silenced the slanderers.

Co-operative influence and convictions are perhaps most evident in rural areas. Still fresh in the author's memory is a visit one frowsy April day to Lapua, where Finland fought one of her bloodiest battles against the

Russian invaders in 1809, now a flourishing village in one of the most fertile and best-cultivated parts of Finland. In the middle of the village stands the stately local authority offices, turreted like a castle, rough cast, with café and restaurant and other social amenities. Through the village runs the old main road, now a broad highway; along both sides lie the business premises, for the most part co-operative institutions of one kind or another. The parish boasts a population of 14,000, practically all co-operators.

There are in the parish three consumer co-operative societies, two S.O.K., one K.K., with ten shops amongst them, seven co-operative creameries, six co-operative Credit Banks, a score of bull societies, threshing societies, pig-breeding societies, and, in intimate relation to agricultural co-operative undertakings, eight farmers' guilds, young farmers' clubs, and other mutual improvement associations. Lapuan Osuuskauppa (Co-operative Retail Society), which, with its capacious stores, occupies a substantial brick building in the middle of the village, sells grocery and provisions, drapery and furnishings, boots and shoes, household utensils, feeding stuffs, manures, agricultural machinery and requirements, and markets yearly for its members many thousands of pounds' worth of grain and other produce. Special show-rooms for agricultural machinery, with large display windows, have been built, and at the railway station the society has its own granary with mechanical conveyers, and cleaning and grading machinery. The society has 1,350 members and an annual turnover of £67,200.

Some miles from Lapua lies the village of Ilmajoki. Just outside the local museum, a mile or so from the church, is a fortress-like monument to Ilkka, Finland "Wallace", the foretime champion of Finnish freedom. Not far away stands the *modern* monument to independence, Ilmajoki consumer co-operators' reassuring headquarters, with a fine range of shops and display of farm machinery, and a model silo at the nearby railway station.

All through the Swedish-speaking Österbotten the same picture meets the eye. In their limpid Swedish, managers and members relate with pride the splendid progress of their societies, and, mid in the village, and often close by the co-operative shop, sounds in corroboration the din of milk-churns from the co-operative creamery, where steam-engines pant and separators purr, in spotless concrete-floored factories.

Time: a few days later; scene: the delegate general meeting of the prosperous Voima consumer co-operative in Tammerfors. Four hours of admirable and relevant discussion of management and business by representatives of various classes and different political parties: Social Democrat, Communist, Liberal. Milk distribution is severely criticised, production problems examined, and whether dividend shall be 1, 1½, or 2 per cent. debated.

Good-tempered, witty, helpful speeches, and, in the heat of the milk-fray, an armistice for a cup of coffee. Members are elected to the Delegate Council on political lists, but no politics of any kind intrude on the discussion. All are anxious to keep the annual meeting to its proper purpose: an assembly for consideration of the affairs of a joint business undertaking. And agreement is finally reached on every point.

Yet another recollection: Valio's annual meeting in the old Students' Hostel in Helsingfors. Sturdy peasant types from all over Finland; short, shrewd, black-eyed Karelians, buirdly Tavastlanders, thriving Österbotteners in wellingtons. The Vasa march is sung and the meeting gets quickly under weigh with a discussion on the most important item in the accounts—expenses. Valio's chief merit has been its vast superiority in selling methods over all its rivals—an eminence not reached without outlay ventured and reflected in charges, which, however, steadily diminish as business is won. But some still grudge their height.

The fluctuations of butter prices and the various influences affecting the world markets are debated with an intimacy on every hand that is astonishing. Explanations are asked and given of various items of expense and their significance. Women take prominent part, but then, 90 per cent. of the prizewinners at Valio's annual competitions for dairy management are women operators.

A middle-aged lady, sitting near, interprets Finnish for the author, and changes from one tongue to the other without a moment's hesitation or difficulty—a fairly common accomplishment in Finland. All is sensible, to the point; no gesticulation, no strained or ornate eloquence, but facts and figures, huge, impregnable.

Perhaps the real reason of the great success achieved is to be found in this same calm, sober, matter-of-fact attitude of Finnish co-operators. Utopian schemes are regarded askance, the solution of the economic problem is simple, honest, straightforward self-help. No claim is urged for co-operative support except on the ground of manifest superiority in final service over all competitors. Finnish co-operation considers itself a form of combination of effort, calculated to raise the output capacity of labour and to ensure the democratic development of the country.

What has already been accomplished, briefly described here, is yet sufficient to afford example and encouragement to the co-operators and the poor of every land, and conviction of the natural and inherent power of the co-operative idea has permeated all ranks, and has ripened into a responsible, yet not arrogant "co-operative spirit". And in that lies the strength and the hope of co-operation in Finland.

Another contributory factor is the readiness with which agreement can be reached and forces assembled. Risk of division and consequent unnecessary multiplication of effort are unhappily increased in post-war Finland, with its recent sanguinary Civil War, its many acute differences of language, politics, and social creed, still far from reconciled, which makes more surprising the paucity of schism that has troubled the co-operative movement. Only in consumer co-operation has there been a split of any moment. Quarrel and dispute have been successfully avoided in defining the limits and boundaries of the various kinds of co-operation—no light task in all the circumstances. Remarkably distinct and clear, these have been of inestimable advantage to co-operation's progress. Specialisation and collaboration have been effectively combined. In comparison, for example, with Denmark, the scheme of organisation of co-operation in Finland is singularly simple and smooth and sound. For this the original impulse and direction have been largely responsible. The strong aversion to any "overlapping" appeals to the foreigner as another augury of still further success.

The careful retention of democratic control is also highly commendable. That Professor Gebhard should, from the outset, have recognised the priceless value of such control does equal credit to his vision and his intelligence. He insisted on its incorporation in every constitution he helped to draft, and never abated his zeal and demand for its maintenance.

Although, quite properly, experts and specialist managers take charge of the daily routine, supreme control and final decision still rests through the Supervisory Council and the Delegate Council on the farmers and workers, who are the mainstay of the business. These representatives, chosen because of their intimate acquaintance and sympathy with the desires and needs of the masses, are responsible for the broad lines of development along which the movement proceeds and for the objects towards which it strives.

But no foolish, irritating check is imposed on the management, nor is their initiative cramped so long as representatives are kept posted as to intention and desire, and careful preliminary trial is guaranteed. Such consultation and confidence are the more sought and prized since the leaders and managers themselves come mainly from the masses.

Co-operation in Finland seems certainly very partial to University-trained men and experts for leading positions, but the conclusion is not, therefore, to be drawn that interests other than true co-operative intrude. The explanation is that, with the possible exception of Norway, within the author's experience, Finland is, at any rate, the Northern country with the highest proportion of peasant and working-class students, and very many of the M.A.s and doctors active in co-operative management are of such origin.

The statement is made, and appears fully justified, that experts who have risen from the ranks in Finland aspire with a kind of home-sickness to co-operative employment, so as to return to and serve in security and comfort their own kin and its interests, even though the pecuniary reward should be less. In any case, there invariably exist friendly and even cordial relations between management and members. Equally certainly, while democratic control has been completely retained, so as to present a notable feature on every hand, there has never been any difficulty in securing experts and specialists for co-operation, due in part, as indicated, to the spread of higher education. All of which strengthens enormously the co-operative structure.

Thus co-operation in Finland is not fickly floating on transient favourable conditions of a day, but is firmly rooted in circumstances peculiar to the country and closely adapted to national traits and needs. So only is to be explained its strength and commanding position in public esteem; but co-operation in Finland is not so nationally peculiar that other lands may not learn therefrom a great deal of practical value in the way of co-operative development. In days to come other peoples will assuredly have much regard to Finland's co-operative progress and prowess, and be eager to learn their lessons.

INDEX

Date Due

Mr 13 '40	Reserved	OCT 15 1952	
Ap 22 '40	History	RESERVED	
My 6 '40		AUG 12 1953	
D 8 '40	SE 21 '48	RESERVED	
Ja 25 '43	RESERVED		
Jl 21 '43	History		
Reserved	115		
History	AG 26 '49		
115	RESERVED		
Reserved	HISTORY		
History	115		
116			
Reserved	SE 28 '50		
History	RESERVED		
115-16			
	SE 4 '51		
RESERVED			
History	RESERVED		
115-116			